Extraordinary Inner Light

Poetry on Healing Trauma
& Realigning with Self

EILEEN ANNE

To A, B, and C, even a book of words could never encompass my love for you.

Table of Contents

Chapter 1 - Healing Trauma — 11

In Release — 13
The Letdown — 15
From the Treetops — 15
Lightening — 16
Who Loved Me Then? — 17
Beam of Light — 22
The Estuary — 25
The Language of the Universe — 28
Wilted Flower — 30
Spirit Guides — 31
Leo Moon — 33
Persist — 36
Murky Waters — 40
Sanctuary — 42
Heart-Shaped Rocks — 44
Blue — 45
Right Beside — 46
When You Became My Angel Guide — 47
Wading in the Mud — 48
Waves of Grief — 48
Lilacs — 49
Pain Reframed — 51
For All I Thought I Was — 52

Chapter 2 - Father & Mother Wound — 53

Father Wound — 55
Swerve — 57
We Aren't Alike — 58
Burnt Popcorn — 60
Nothing into Something — 62
Hanging Up — 65
The Voice I Have Now — 66
Words to the Wind — 67
The Puppeteer — 68
Not There Yet — 71
From Where I Stood — 72
Return to Strangers — 74
In-Between — 76
The Storm of You — 77
Long Before — 78
Someone I Knew — 79

Through My Dreams, I Heal	*80*
Lower the Pedestal	*81*
Passing You	*82*
Greatness	*84*
Gently Looking Back	*85*
Reset	*86*
One Last Thing	*87*

Chapter 3 - Breaking Previous Patterns — **89**

Rebuilding	*91*
Broken Clock	*92*
Shifting	*92*
This Again	*92*
Alchemy	*93*
Cycle-Breaker	*96*
From the Wind	*98*
Scribbles	*99*
Backlog	*100*
Mirrored Water	*102*
Yellowed Pages	*102*
Letting Go	*103*
Softening	*103*
Crosswalk	*104*
Goodbye Fear	*105*
Present	*106*
Innermost	*107*
Not Who I Was	*108*
Voiceless	*109*
I'm So Over You	*111*
Ancient History	*112*
Spiritual Math	*113*
The Pause	*114*
Cutting Cords	*114*
Healing Hearts	*115*
Programming	*116*
Lanterns in the Sky	*118*
Breaking Free	*119*

Chapter 4 - Realizing Self-Worth — **121**

My Light	*123*
A Little Bit	*123*
I Was Told	*124*
My Shelter	*125*
Some Body	*126*
Learning to Love Myself	*128*

Loving Yourself Deeper	*130*
Pure Love	*131*
Never Me	*132*
The World Does Revolve Around You	*134*
If You Could See Yourself	*135*
Honoring Yourself	*136*
I Stand Tall	*138*
The Girl on the Timeline	*140*
1,111	*142*
Palm Trees Make Me Cry	*143*
It's Time	*144*
Love, Then & Now	*145*
What She Deserves	*146*
Be Brave	*147*
E.) All of the Above	*150*

Chapter 5 - Awakening Divine Feminine — **151**

Broken Scales	*153*
Emerging	*155*
Remembered Woman	*156*
Generations Before and After	*158*
A Drop of Water	*159*
Motherhood	*159*
Little Flowers	*160*
Mama Math	*161*
Colors of Joy	*162*
Awakening	*163*
My Mama Heart	*163*
There's Room for Both	*164*
Just a Moment	*165*
Mama, You Don't Come Last	*166*
Bon Voyage	*169*
Heart Wall	*171*
Redefining Relationships	*172*
Fatigued	*173*
Wise Woman	*176*
Higher Octaves	*178*
Green Rosaries	*179*
Though We Never Met	*182*
I Will Carry You Again	*184*
Mama Elle	*186*
My Mother	*188*
A Decade for Me	*189*
Great Goddess	*190*
Goddess Lineage	*194*

Chapter 6 - Stepping into Oneself — 195

- Sunday School — *197*
- The Power of Writing — *197*
- Living Bigger — *198*
- This Comfy Space — *200*
- Armor — *201*
- Realign with Self Era — *202*
- Mold — *204*
- The Empath's Return — *207*
- Higher Self — *208*
- Squeaky Floor — *209*
- Did You Know? — *214*
- Wheels of Energy — *215*
- Within Myself — *215*
- Showers of Love — *216*
- Full Self — *217*
- The First Time I Felt Peace — *218*
- Life in Shapes — *219*
- Deeper — *220*
- Earth School — *222*
- Let the Goodness In — *223*
- Light Language — *224*
- Saturn — *225*
- Red Camaro in the Sky — *226*
- Your Strength — *227*
- The Artist Across — *228*
- Soul's Gold — *229*
- Be Still — *230*
- Honoring It All — *231*
- Undefinable — *231*
- Symphony of Light — *232*
- My Life, My Light — *233*
- The Essence of Becoming — *234*

Chapter 7 - Connecting to Nature & Greater — 235

- Tuning In — *237*
- Winding Roads — *239*
- Half-Moon — *240*
- Surrender — *240*
- Light Beings in the Magical Forest — *241*
- The Deva of Roses — *244*
- Deep in the Forest — *244*
- Held by Nature — *245*
- The Ancient Forest — *246*
- No Worries — *247*

My Tree	248
From the Leaves	248
Healing	249
Feathers of Blue	250
Flowing with the River	251
Lowcountry	252
This Rocky Plane	253
The Night Sky	254
Sacred Shapes	256
Not to Dim	257
The Only Language I Speak	257
Cosmic Dust	258
Sweet Dreams	258
Who We Are	259
My Boy	260
My Girl	260
One with Faeries	261
Rainbow Light	262
Remembering	263
Inner Child	264
Meeting Again	265
Who I've Been, Who I Am	269
Divine Grid	270
Rising Up	271
The Last to Know	271
Extraordinary Inner Light	272

Acknowledgments 274

About the Author 277

Praise for *Extraordinary Inner Light* 279

1

Healing Trauma

*I take the lessons
just as I take the blessings—
feeling it all flow.*

In Release

Here I am
writing again
just as I was after you left

Finding solace
in the words deep within me

Pulling out emotions
so they don't settle within

If I could rewind and spend time
letting out what didn't need to stay

When I poured my heart onto the page
to bypass the conversations I couldn't engage

When I gathered all the unwanted emotion
and stored it, letting its weight
pile on and on until I tipped,

Into the dead tangled branches
the overgrown weeds,
the poison ivy growing up the poplar tree
reminiscent of the one I climbed when young,

Never getting past the first branch—
for years I clung
dangling like the old sloth

The hibernation is over
a harvest of some sort, a collection of
what's ready to go, so this land can be cleared and re-sowed
with something beautiful, not something heavy or lost—
a thousand scattered oak trees
draped in the most enchanting moss

True transformation without disguise
if you look into the phoenix's sapphire eyes,
the magnitude of what was held
quite heavy to unleash,
but little by little it's propelled
as my words tumble out,
my feelings have no choice, but to reroute,
the lessons kept coming until it was time
to let go, to move out, to brave the feelings I couched,

That's the beauty, I suppose,
time is an illusion juxtaposed

I thought I missed the shortcuts,
I thought I took great lengths,
what seemed to be the long way around actually connects
bringing me full circle as I reflect,
I didn't miss my turn, I wasn't in the wrong place,
but I can't live in joy holding feelings I can't face

So let's transmute the pain into a beautiful flow of words
ones that want to be heard, ones that heal the world

You're guiding the light, shining on your shadows,
starting within and going from there, soul's growth,
clearing a path through the forest,
transforming the meadows,
flowing with what comes up,

And on it goes,
on it goes.

The Letdown

The day the tears stopped,
I vowed I would never cry again
nineteen years the habit ran deep
I only showed my happy side, buried the truth
in the depth of my cells— symptom after symptom,
my body communicating that this wasn't working well

Now I'm taking the containers down one at a time,
like old boxes on dusty shelves that once filled the garage
as I feel the emotion powerfully collect
the tears stream down my cheeks like the first time,
surrender, don't suppress, feel, don't resist—
uncage the colors held with every tear,
every uncomfortable emotion,
knowing the skies will clear

I don't need to hold onto the rain until it storms.

From the Treetops

There is a thing called baggage following us around
heavy and shameful, it feels like a major downfall
yet there's a different view if you spin around,
looking from the treetops rather than the ground
it's not baggage you carry at arm's length,
instead, you carry badges of strength—
what you perceived as your darkest hour
can be turned into an incredible superpower.

Lightening

What if I told you your grief wasn't meant to be carried,
it wasn't meant to be slung in a knapsack across your back
as you hunch over, losing sight of everything
but the dirt you walk upon, the enormity of your load
constantly weighing and weakening on your body,
your mind, but not your soul... your soul knows,

Your soul knows this life wasn't meant to be spent
looking at your toes

What if I told you that it wasn't just your grief you carried,
yet others' grief as well, in those heartbreaking moments
where you wanted to take away their pain... you did,
into your knapsack it went, as it got heavier and heavier,
tearing holes in the very thing that gave it a home,

Why is it easier to wrap it up and carry it with us,
to patch the holes and put a broken-hearted bow on it,
rather than to sit down and sift through it?

The magnitude of the task feels like the enormity of the load,
but they are not equal, for far too long, we've carried too much,
too much of our own, too much that doesn't belong,
too much from generations before

It's time to put down what wasn't meant to be carried,
to sort the clutter, observe what comes through,
feel what comes up, release what's ready to go

To stand up again, this time taller,
lighter, freer than before,

We can love what we lost
without it being so heavy.

Who Loved Me Then?

Aches in my hands and legs return,
instead of trying to will the pain away
I let the symptoms take me back
to the overwhelming emotion
I stored long before

In a safe place
where I felt loved and taken care of,
I returned to the girl who wandered the streets alone,
nameless and bleak, and oh-so-full of grief
for what she lost without any direction to go

Who ate ice cream and French fries at 3am to numb
when the bottom of the glass didn't do the trick,
once the tears did come, there was no end

Alleyways dark and damp,
hallowing down the antiquated cobblestone,
the laughter of others cut so deep
I was supposed to be laughing along

Truly alone
no one had any answers
no one had anything to give worthy of receipt
who was left to love me?

The words
that came from the elders' mouths,
conditions on what they doled out

The moving truck pulling away,
heavy boxes filled-to-the-brim
with nothing

The last time I saw him
I pulled my suitcase through the grass—
one loving hug before departure,
mine, but really his

A different continent
no one knowing my heart
no one checking up on me
no one seeing if I was okay—
who loved me then?

I roamed the cold, rainy streets
drenched in grief as the church bells ring,
all the Sunday masses couldn't have prepared me,
my tears sting, no example, no mentor
elders who suppressed, how was I to process?
a complicated problem of calculus,
where the explanation didn't exist

I looked for love in places it didn't reside
I looked for comfort where there wasn't—
trying different things to cope but nothing fit
weeping my way through the cities of Europe,
my dreams were puddles collected on the road
it wasn't supposed to be like this

In search of someone to really listen,
not someone who didn't respect me to start
not someone whose service project I was—
be nice to the girl with the broken heart,
not someone who turned their head and thought
one less problem for me to worry about

In search of someone to okay my feelings
so I could cry or kick or scream out of grief,
sadness, loss, instead, I felt I had to be—
strong for others, doing well,

I couldn't fall back even though there was nowhere to go
the ground didn't get lower or colder,
the bottom of the hole

I just stayed there
apologizing for being sad,
for being a burden, for not having it together,
waiting for a savior, a rescuer,
someone stronger to pull me out,
not understanding how I was storing
my feelings like an old memory book—
one way in, no way out

Then came the symptoms—
physical and emotional intertwined
one not existing without the other by its side,
I thought if I kept busy and moving
and kept my mind occupied
then the volume would eventually subside

It was always there as the years flashed,
photos still stored until an old symptom comes up
and takes me right back,
I return to an old version of myself
to finally, safely let go
to face what I didn't before,
the tough feelings, the hard questions
one that plagued my present mind—
who loved me then?

And my mind goes blank—
although there's love now
I feel it so deeply every day,
when I go back to release what was stored
I can't help but wonder: who loved her?

Silence extends as
thorns grow from pain, grief, loss,
a wild mess that couldn't be wrangled—
the decades flash, when at last
a beautiful pink rose appeared,
from this pallid plant cast to the side
no one expecting color again

The wall of thorns protected my sacred space
if no one loved me at my lowest
how could I trust again?

And so,
it came time to weed the garden
scale back its walls, trim the overgrown,
the offshoots, the beautiful parts,
releasing the past
reshaping what was left
no longer sad for myself,
joy for this beautiful life that came after
but to fully step into what comes next,
it's time to close this chapter

Picking through the pile of trimmings,
taking one last trip to the past
with a handful of pink roses begotten from pain,
handing them to the girl walking alone
pink petals bring color to the monochrome,
her eyes meet mine and she knows
a gift from the future bestowed
the beautiful rose,
its petals layered to unfold
revealing one simple message—

You are loved by all divinity,
that's how these blossoms came to be

Dropping pink petals along her path,
the angels join leaving signs for her to find,
when you leap along the timeline
returning to the places you lingered in your mind,
giving a nudge, a sign, a symbol, your love,
forward movement may just come,
igniting the thorns of yesterday
watching them light and glow,
release of the old pain into orange, yellow, indigo

Then, turn to ashes, thanking it all,
softening the sadness
knowing you can move on,
the old image is simply a stop along the way
transforming the old with the rose bouquet,
showing the blessings to come
revealing the messages of love—
the gap no longer there,

I was never without,
I've always been loved.

Beam of Light

I hold the memory of the last time I saw you
in the deepest chambers of my heart,
as if wrapped with gauze,
mummified, but alive to me

Wearing it like a gold locket
I never took off
nor opened for anyone else,
though it's time to share
in remembrance,
in release,

I left our childhood home to study abroad
I'd waited my life for independence,
the joy I would finally experience
hopping on and off planes,
checking countries off my bucket list,
not knowing you were at the end of yours

But you knew
as I pulled my suitcase through the grass
fighting with gravity as my anxiety rose,
our father hollering from the running car in the road
before the three-hour ride to BWI,
trying to hurry, so he didn't explode

You called after me with haste in your voice,
saying my name in a way I never heard before
my ears perked as I turned, watching as you ran
frantic down the brick walkway:

You left without saying goodbye, you called to me,
and I couldn't place the difference in your voice
but no one ever left home for months at time
or had dreams as big as mine, so I wrote it off,

but my intuition knew
there was a reason
you needed to hug me tight one last time

I left my purse, I was coming right back,
you avoided my eyes as I spoke,
you stretched out your arms
and I nestled my head in your chest,
for as long as you would allow—
happy and content that you were
wishing me well,
I wasn't emotional
I didn't shed a tear
rather I reveled in the moment
I had long waited for

You pulled away, I let go
our father now honking the horn,
our mother peeping at the exchange
from the bay window

Our final goodbye
before my departure,
but really it was yours

Two weeks later, my phone rang in Ireland—
you were gone before I flew home,
my suitcase didn't get stuck
no one was calling after me
the grief overshadowed me

You were my first friend,
my brother, my protector
the only masculine
I could remotely look up to,
the first boy I put on a pedestal
like when I was in sixth grade, you in eighth,

we both had roles in Peter Pan:
I was a lost boy (though I thought myself a Wendy)
and you backstage shining the lights
as I danced and sang—
together but separate,
not so different as we are now

The tears still stream
but my heart is healing as I unwrap the gauze
that kept your memory protected for all these years,
after your departure

Heaven knew when you arrived
the grand work you'd be doing from the skies,
you're high in the lightroom again
shining on me—
guiding, lighting, cheering
together, but separate,
a beam of light connecting us
Eileen and Dennis,
just as we were before

And, the Universe winks
her clever imagery weaved,
the most beautiful embroidery one has ever seen
her way of soothing, connecting, guiding
softening the karmic lessons of our time,
but showing the connection between two souls never dies.

The Estuary

You left me
to fend for myself
not even an afterthought,
I was still alive yet
you let me go too

Into no man's land
where not a soul knew me,
sometimes I wonder if you thought
I was strong and resilient
but really, your load lightened
while mine got heavier

Overseas, alone,
cold, heavy, empty,
a never-ending shower of grief,
no warmth to come even
with so many layers

Looking closely
the tears fell uncontrollably
for months I couldn't stop them

I walked along the Irish riverbank
bundled in the grief of a thousand coats,
as my stream of tears joined the tributary
floating away with my hope

I slid on goggles as I free-fell in the Alps
face-to-face with magical terrain,
but tears blurred my vision
as they created rain

I tossed coins into the Italian fountain
sealing the promise I'd be here again,
but my tears splashed back
reminders of the state I was in

I tried to keep moving
onward with my dreams,
as if the trauma of grief
didn't surround me,
yet my body couldn't move on
with my soul screaming out

The tears were messengers
telling me this was too big
to keep stuffing down, nevertheless,
I continued to functionally suppress
until the tears stopped appearing

Yet they reemerged
on random drunken nights,
they reemerged in the depths
of my darker-than-ever eyes,
they reemerged in the form of
chronic illness

Seventeen years pass
and as with the rising of the sun,
the depths of my soul know
this no longer serves

As the current comes in,
it feels unnerving and startling,
weren't the waters so warm and calm,
chaos and ailments became my norm,
easier to stay in the known, even when painful,
rather than move to the unknown

My body, mind, and soul intertwine
sending me the message that it's time
for me to give rise
to what I didn't need to hold—
layers to unravel, the same layers
that kept me bundled
no longer served a purpose

Divinity surrounds me,
raises me up with angelic wings,
protected, surrounded, loved,
I dip in the waters
slowly and carefully
deeper and deeper
letting the waves come through—
soppy, sudsy, turbulent, serene,
not hidden, not ignored, not diluted,
flowing and feeling into what was
held in for so long

Giving my mind and body the grace
and space they needed for healing to come,
sift through the pain of all I held,
knowing I am wrapped in overflowing love

Safe for me to let the trauma release,
never to reemerge, never to reappear
to be transmuted into something beautiful

Strong and resilient, I'm here at last
as I watch the waves slowly roll away,
with eyes much lighter than before.

The Language of the Universe

After he died
I was filled with so many
feelings I didn't know how to feel

Months of grieving
the Universe brought me solace
in the form of you

When I was moments from collapsing
from the weight of it all
you rescued me

Our eyes locked
and I knew we had met
lifetimes ago

I held all of myself out
muddled piles of paint on a palette,
you dipped your brush, ignored the mess
and together we created the most beautiful art

That's what this Universe does,
brings the magic back when we need it most

Safe and loved, I reveled in the bliss
the Universe so graciously gave

We walked the wooden bridge together,
and I grew stronger
in love and laughter
I found my light again

Yet it wasn't an always,
just a *for-now*, two souls saying goodbye,
stones added to the labyrinth of this lifetime

I long-carried that story of you
sensationalized all that was,
equated you with the rescue,
the heartfelt tow when I was stuck
on the side of the road

And then, life beat me down again
I longed for you to strengthen,
to tell me I didn't deserve this,
to help me make it across again

And that's when the Universe gave
the next lesson—a solo journey,

Working through the darkness,
I found flickers of light—
inner strength, peace, divine trust,
following these glimmers,
as dim as they were at times,
into the next bright clearing

Turning back to the old bridge
I crossed on my own,
I watch my reflection rise with the water,

The Universe, my wise teacher,
stole away my scaffolding
for the most magical
thing of all—

I met myself.

Wilted Flower

Do you only see me as the wilted flower?
not strong enough to stand on my own,
who needs to depend upon—
the stronger, the smarter,
the brighter to carry me through?

Whose brokenness precedes me
whose sadness is seen in my wide eyes,
do you only see me for my brokenness—
and what happens when I become strong?

Will I wilt again as that's the pattern I know,
or will I stand in my power realizing
there's more for me than I ever knew?
I was never the wilted flower you saw
I was never the wilted flower I felt I was

I carried your perception of me,
my empathic gifts crossing the lines
confusing your thoughts with mine

Staying small, a fraction of who I could be,
unable to see, if turned my face to the sun
instead of the shadow, I could start to receive
and really grow

Roots deeper than ever before, new blossoms begin to form
reaching up toward the heavens so I always remember

There's nothing fragile or broken about me,
nor the flower, she's born of joy and strength
and if her petals begin to wilt,
she can let the old fade away
as she turns toward goodness,
letting the blessings come in to stay

It's time to show my strength
the words I whisper to myself,
I say them loud and let them be known
I am complete and whole
I am complete and whole
standing tall in love and joy
my petals begin to unfold.

Spirit Guides

Oh, Fairy Godmother, heal my unhealed parts
turn my grief to volcanic ash,
sparkles and glimmers—
wishing it worked like that, but
healing from the inside out is a rocky footpath

The tears flood as I process the notion,
to release long-carried pain, all the emotion,
it needs to be felt again
and not stored or stuffed or cached;
these patches simply won't last,

Like the shadow cast by the bobcat,
no matter how lightly he treads
how stealthily he sneaks
his shadow still behind,
like the emotional burden that extends
as I ignored the messages my body sent—
delivered but not received,
now the pain is coming up again
this time to heal as it peaks

For a girl who loves a plan
my page feels blank, my mind spins
no action steps beyond
longing for a magic wand,
tears puddle in my eyes,
and there's my answer in the water—
I'm resisting, fighting against the natural waves,
instead of bobbing up and down
or, better yet, floating along

To surrender and let it flow
even when uncomfortable
knowing the pain won't last
knowing it's resurfacing to leave
knowing I'm always being guided,
the ancestors and godmothers inside of me

To listen, to be still, to let be,
a simple reset of me
to remember time in the shade
won't last forever—
a leveling up,
an upgrade.

Leo Moon

Betrayal isn't talked about enough;
its connotation twisted up
linked to petty gossip
like your best friend stealing your crush
when really betrayal hits deep in the gut—
coming from someone supposed to love you
it can really mess you up,
damaging your self-worth
leaving you feeling like you aren't enough,
living your life not knowing who to trust
or if you are giving out too much?

Then there's the shaming,
the inner voice on repeat:
how could you have missed the signs?
how could you be so dense? they got you
on a blindside, right where it hurts the worst,
your scene blurred, when all you did
was love too hard

There are stages of betrayal, just like grief,
as it messes with our minds
because our reality wasn't intertwined
with what was right before our eyes

I was so eager for love from all I lost
I couldn't spot the difference
'til I was double-crossed,
the shame, the guilt, the self-blame,
judgment from myself
all the education under my belt,
all the things I perceive that others miss
yet I'm somehow I was ill-equipped,
when it came to trusting you
how was I your fool?

I believed all you said until I saw otherwise—
my flooded eyes, your slandering words
a 180 from what I just heard, needing to rewire my brain
to know what a smile doesn't mean
to know not everyone is a safe space,
lock and key, I thought this was behind me
but it returns in the form of fluff—
the facades, the grins, the hugs, and apparently
that's enough to deceive

I've always loved words, I speak in metaphors,
not to mention my alliteration,
but my blind spot is your words of affirmation
they go straight to my heart, open too wide,
not stopping to realize the intention behind
my tolerance for you was sky-high
when my own well of self-compassion was dry

It wasn't a fair fight; it never was
but every time you walked through my door
with a smile on your face and a cold embrace
intuitively I knew this wasn't right,
but you said you loved me
and when I use those words, I mean them
I didn't know there was an option B

My heart feels fragile, worn leathered skin
ready to crack at all the bends
from too much washing my hands clean of you—
your narcissistic ways, your toxic relations,
we are over and will never be again but
I forgot there are other wolves in sheep's clothing,
a lesson too hard to learn with you,
so it will come in gentler ways for healing
which is what these tears are

I've got my mirrors on
seeing back and forward, side-to-side
I won't be anyone's fool again—
another lesson of my time,
words don't always mean,
smiles don't always translate,
can't get swept up in compliments,

My Leo moon softened too soon,
connecting inward and proceeding with caution
the worst part of betrayal is how delicate
my heart feels, out of tune,
knowing all the love it holds
didn't mean a thing to you

I'll pick up the pieces; I always do
but I can't put them back together
instead, I'll hold the remnants as a reminder
that sometimes things have to break to release
the old energy that was stuck,

While my heart feels like it split
all those cracks and tints
there's actually more space—
new avenues I can trace
to let self-love aggregate.

Persist

Toes on the coffee table,
I beg you to rub my feet
you ask why I'm always achy;
from living, I reply, oblivious,
not realizing I was living with chronic illness

At twenty-three, I rationed my energy
though teachers expected on their feet,
my calves would ache
the joints in my hands and fingers would throb
I'd crack my bones for relief,
but none was ever brought

My arms were always sore
I'd feel as if I lifted all night long,
but the only gym I saw
was the sign from Route 1

Maybe I'd held the steering wheel wrong
maybe it was the way I slept
I'd rationalize my pain
trying to find what I could correct

Never finding the root,
always in the sky, branches reaching out
a disconnect to my feet—nothing grounding me

I'd sleep away Saturday
rising at noon to eat takeout
on the couch before falling right back
I get up early during the week;
my job is intense, it takes a lot out

The smallest activities drained me
I'd work up all my energy to rise
to wash dishes, pull weeds
before retreating to the HQ,
(otherwise known as the couch) where
my eyes glazed and I'd check out

I slept every long car ride
even after a full night's sleep—
my body would heat up
yet I was always within normal range
nothing quantitative, just my pain

My throat would ache as if I
swallowed a fish bone; my voice never strong,
medicine over and over to suppress
even the cycle stressed

I was living with functional illness,
I could turn on and push through
but when I let go, every symptom screamed

When I pushed myself too far—
a normal day for most—I could feel every nerve in my body,
the aches were that intense, down to the hair follicles on my head
the fatigue would overtake, I'd cry in weakness and pain
no longer a newlywed, sometimes I couldn't even walk to bed

The doctors couldn't see, never found anything wrong with me
a merry-go-round of *well, you look fine to me*
I cried in every office while they ran their numbers, did their tests—
the nurse told me I was too pretty to act so sick

Add my folks to the list of those who didn't believe,
you look great, they'd say and call me names behind my back—
hypochondriac

Some can't have empathy for others unless
they're in your shoes but to constantly deny someone's reality?
that's emotional abuse, messing with my head
maybe I am fine, I thought, it's all I ever heard

So I learned to live with my weaknesses
hiding my symptoms so as to not be judged
and making accommodations for myself,
what I could do and couldn't
before I needed rest, making lifestyle
changes that seemed best
nothing fixed, but I got better at living
with chronic illness

A decade now passed, new mom fatigue
they rationalized my exhaustion
or asked me if I was depressed—
recovering from difficult birth,
I pushed for more tests

A thyroid diagnosis
sky-high for someone as young as me
still, they turned their heads and said,
just some inflamed nodes
it's not a big deal until you're older
years of gaslighting finally wore me down
maybe I'm just weak, maybe I can't tolerate
the pain of life like others do?

New mama back at work—
maybe if my mind remains occupied
I couldn't linger on the pain,
black mold in the school's radiators
brought new symptoms to my invisible list,
here I am just a mom trying to live her best
unknowingly caught in the throes of chronic illness

I eventually caved
and rested and took care of myself
and let other people's opinions return to dirt
transmuted by Mother Earth into healing
and love for myself

Decades late, a diagnosis arrives:
autoimmune disease, illness deep
within my cells causing excessive fatigue

Now when the symptoms return,
I'm in disbelief I lived like this—
every day I thought myself weak
fragile, less-than, when the pain
I've endured only shows my strength

To all those whose voices weren't heard
who felt unseen, unrecognized
who felt lost in a system that was
supposed to support them

I see you
I hear you
I have so much love for you

Look back and say those words
to yourself over and over and over
and as the tears fall, so does the weight
of what you carried,

Just as the wind blows
and the chimes start twisting and playing
there's beauty in pain
finding the lessons
learning from them
and moving forward even on days you're in bed

So long as you remember
You are seen
You are loved
You are heard
You are understood

Here I am, year twenty from the start
releasing old toxins,
the emotional burden of centuries
and I'm finally strong enough to share my story,
to know that my symptoms aren't me,
to know that all who denied my reality
aren't a reflection of what I felt,
of what I hold in me.

Murky Waters

I spent years trying to avoid the darkness,
the depths of chronic illness,
the heavy fog always lurked behind me
if I stayed positive then I wouldn't be caught in it,
yet night always came surrounded by heavy clouds
ridden with fear, wondering if I would see the sun again

Thrown into the dark pools where I couldn't stand
nor see my feet, I found things I'd never see in the light,
darkness has a way of uncovering all
we've been silently carrying, avoiding, overlooking

Down the dusty steps of my childhood basement
I couldn't reach the light switch, crept without so much a flashlight,
I settled into the brown plaid chair that held my tears
after the wasp stings, bruised knees, the brokenness, the fears,
my eye catches the Uno cards left, *draw two*
didn't mean you sketch, holding in my voice,
afraid to speak up, never flipping the right switch,
unfinished dreams from the generation before
abandoned like an old boxcar,
the trauma of those that departed,
scaling the shadowed streets solo,
the sorrow I carried from others
because it hurt to see them suffer,
the lack of compassion I gave myself
because I used it all out on others,
living in the in-between,
not fully me and not who you wanted me to be—
pure abandonment of self,

Like the oil paintings I once adored
looking through the faux window at the snowy scene
how I admired the artist's techniques,
always looking outward, never within,
built up and torn down,
the guilt for staying when my heart was unaligned

The green knit blanket, made by hand—
obligation not love, wrapping myself in it
one last time,
the darkness helped me see
all the places that needed healing,
the darkness showed me
I can't go forward while backpedaling,
the darkness gave me gifts
as I learned how to release,
the darkness showed me how
to honor my body as sacred never weak,
the darkness showed me how
going back to once unsafe places
can bring me full circle, the last stop on the train
is the same as the first,
in the depth of the night,
the cold breath I see swirl from my lips,
waiting for the train's headlight to appear,
so I can climb on and feel the warmth of leaving here

Sitting in the darkness gave me the resolve to find the light,
I need not fear what was already there
I have the strength to move forward, the will to heal,
old emotions and memories can go safely from here,
revisited with a lens of healing
I don't need to carry the ancient stories with me
the darkness showed me what the light couldn't,

And so, I sat in the murky waters
and simply let them clear.

Sanctuary

Is this world safe
outside of my own cocoon?
the sanctuary I've created
to bring joy and comfort and safety in
when I couldn't feel it on the outside,

To venture out again
this time stronger and wiser
without the worry of pricking my finger
on the wheel that spins

The worries and fears of past trauma—
a gray cloud that always follows
almost impossible to let joy in

I wasn't meant to live this way—
it's time to face
the parts of myself
I tried to erase

Out I go to find safety
in the quiet path of the woods
knowing I am protected, I have what I need,
the gray cloud is quieter here,

To find safety in the loving embrace of a friend
a wordless exchange, my head held in a way
that remembers what it's like to be nurtured

To find safety where there's dissonance
when voices are raised—
my highly sensitive heart won't be carried away
in the throes of the notes,
feet still on the ground,
I can turn the volume down

Too long I've walked this earth
as if it was me versus the world,
how human of me
to make it a competition
when we co-exist and co-create
with all that surrounds

To know safety is within me,
to know safety is around me,
to know if it starts to feel unsafe again,
I can plug into the sanctuary I've created
within myself, and recharge,
knowing *what's in, is out*
the virtue reflected right back

And if I struggle again
I hope to find kind eyes in the passerby
so they'll remind me that all is okay,
all is right, there's safety on the outside

Like the first stranger I passed
I was fresh from the cocoon
all he did was say hello and ask me how I was,
but his words echoed the goodness
I'd long been searching for.

Heart-Shaped Rocks

When you died, you were the first,
the first I knew to really be gone
I was told to look for the signs—
the birds, the feathers, the butterflies

Your presence was so big in this life,
how could you send me such minuscule signs?
too ordinary, too easily missed
I wanted them louder and clearer

That's the funny thing about humans,
we want everything bigger and better and brighter
and that's the funny thing about other dimensions,
you must get quiet to really hear,
change your lens to really see

And so, hearts appeared:
heart-shaped rocks, heart-shaped leaves,
flower petals overlapping, hearts etched into the trees
the love poured in—
a dozen butterflies around the pool, reminiscent of yours
a robin with plumes the shade of your eyes,
leaving me a path of feathers to my favorite nook outside

Each time overcome with emotion, my eyes filled with tears,
my lens reset, nothing ordinary here,
no second-guessing, the signs are there;
they've always been when I get quiet and clear

Though we were distant here on earth
you sent me a trail of treasure, the start of my connection,
eyes wide open, heart-expanding,
feeling the depths of your presence
in receipt of divine love.

Blue

If depression were a color
I'd paint it blue,
not navy nor cyan
but cerulean to match the ocean, the skies,
my brother's eyes
the tears I've cried

Numbing the pain, afraid
to fall into melancholy
as he did, but
different issues arose—
the sickness from holding on
instead of letting go

Karmic lessons arrived
from his departure,
filling me with dread
instead of gratitude
for what it was, for what I am

I am free to feel,
without the fear of falling,
I am not my feelings
they can roll out,
just as they rolled in

As natural as the blue skies, the ocean,
my brother's eyes, the tears I cried,
I breathe, I breathe
clouds of blue back into the skies.

Right Beside

Your absence is palpable,
leaving the edges of my heart frayed,
and while I have sewn so much back
together in all the time that has passed,
there are still loose strings

Your presence is palpable,
brightening the chambers of my heart,
bringing laughter and love to places
that long been dark, a darkness I never
understood why I always had a broken heart

I was missing love, just as you were—
we grew up without, it played out in different ways,
our paths were always the same,
though we landed in different planes:

For you, the spiritual realm, for me, the human experience
of feeling through the lows and highs—
missing you, while you laugh and wonder
how I can miss someone who is right beside.

When You Became My Angel Guide

I remember the days when I couldn't think about you
without a grand flood—
I played songs on repeat about angels leading you in,
I read your letters over and over, savoring your handwriting
I told all the best stories of you to anyone who would listen
I cherished every snippet of a dream I had with you,
I didn't know how much my heart could hurt
I had to wrap my head around how you really were gone

Now I can think about you and laugh and smile,
knowing in the depths of my soul that you're still with me,
I know the angels led you in because you're one of them
I don't need to read the past, it's rewritten
I don't need to tell your stories, they are already known
I talk with you anytime I please, as you are right beside
I now know how much the human heart can love

You are serving your divine purpose,
just from a different place, our lines no longer intersecting,
now running parallel, but still together, after all this time

One may wonder, *what changed, was it time?*
no, it wasn't time at all, it was feeling, observing,
releasing emotion as it came, deepening my connection,
opening my heart to divinity

The pain doesn't have to stay, it will come in waves to be felt
and released, some days the tide will be gentle and calm
other times it will be turbulent and strong,
knocking us to our knees, feel and release, feel and release,
until we can find balance again in the sand

Can time really heal all wounds?
Depends—depends on how we use our time.

Wading in the Mud

When you carry unprocessed feelings like grief, heartbreak, or sadness, it doesn't matter how much time passes. One week or ten years is all the same. Until you feel and free the emotion, the energy in motion. Yes, it will be messy, but you're already wading in the mud. When you feel, you create the space—little pathways guiding you to more solid ground.

Waves of Grief

I could write a thousand poems
words channeling through my body,
metaphors scrolling my mind
landing in the old backyard,
with the falling fencepost
in need of more than just a log,
I wonder if the grief will ever go

Not just the grief of the loss of another,
but the loss of the previous versions,
loss of what should have felt permanent,
the grief of a lifetime all bundled together
piles of knitted sweaters, hats, and mittens
to protect from the fierce weather

I wonder when the grief will feel less heavy
when my body can free itself
of the extra layers holding me down,
when my cells will grow stronger and mightier
as I once felt before the pain

I come into my body with the intention
to release this wave, like all the others that have left,
crisscross legs in Buddha's pose
soft-knitted whispers as my head sinks into my hands
I push to my edge, feeling and freeing un-comfortability,
it leaves out my toes, grounding down,
until another wave
comes along.

Lilacs

When the pain comes
rather than try to will it away
I breathe into it softly
and ask what it needs

It wants to leave
it wants the release
but something is holding on
keeping that part so tightly wound

Breaking a pattern is tough
when it's so deeply engrained,
little by little I evolve and change
but the pain still signals

For as many years as it's been
communicating with me,
I can't expect a miracle
the minute I start to listen

I've never been patient enough
it must be time to learn,
to exercise that within myself
for the deep-seated, deep-rooted
healing that wants to come

So every day I'll connect
breathing into the pain softly
and asking what it needs
legs-crossed in Buddha pose
listening, meditating
on what comes

Lilacs appear in the mind's eye
to show me I've always been
deserving, and a message comes,
take them and breathe in their essence
as you twirl in joy and love knowing
they were grown for you
even when you thought they weren't
yours to have

Breathe in their fragrance
all the way down to your feet
imagining the violet energy moving
through each chakra center
rebalancing, bringing worth,
abundance, deservingness
to the wheels of energy

Each day I connect
to my parts with love,
remembering they are energy,
they are communicating,
they are working beautifully to heal me.

Pain Reframed

Exploring the gifts
not harboring the pain—
it doesn't need a home within you,
just visiting, let it pass through

For the challenges you've endured
for those you feel wronged you
not falling into victimhood
but seeing it for what it was
roles played
pain reframed into
lessons and gifts

To move through
the karmic lessons you've signed up for in this earthly land
the large emotion brings movement forward
new direction, new choices, new bliss
old patterns falling away if you have the courage to persist

Dreams with your name written across
you'd never thought you'd reach,
but if you can let the trauma process
releasing it from the caverns of your body, your mind,
your soul can wade in the treasure found.

For All I Thought I Was

For all the times I wasn't understood
For all the times I didn't understand
For all the tears I held in
For all the illness they became
For all the ways I didn't understand the world
For all the ways I didn't understand myself
For all the tears that now want to be shed
For all that I was, for all that I am.

2

Father & Mother Wound

I wished I harbored nothing but love, instead I'm trying to forgive.

Father Wound

I always looked for father figures
to give me what you didn't

Sitting at my best friend's family dinners,
feeling seen and appreciated,
kindhearted conversation,
I used to imagine what it would be like
for hers to be mine

Watching afterschool specials,
I imagined John Ritter as my dad,
my heart filled with warmth watching
the love he held, the love he was,
I cried for three days when he died

There were others, a teacher whose compassion
and forgiveness through tragedy
opened my eyes to a new frequency,
a boss, a co-worker, a boyfriend's dad,
those who protected and showed kindness,
and were actually proud

I found what I should have
received from you in other places,

I learned virtues I should have
witnessed from you in other ways,

Fragments that I pieced together
to make me feel whole,
yet, there always was a void,

All the pieces I picked up from different puzzles,
I put them together the best I could,
but I was never complete

The absence of love always preceding,
this non-stop feeling of needing
outside validation to feel
loved and appreciated

Taking a deep dive into my soul
working through the emptiness,
layers of raw pain
I tried to fill

I deserved more than I received,
most know their worth
through parental love,
as natural as the sun above

Yet, I had to discover mine,
a foundation from fragments
until I found what was missing
in myself

I had to realize my worth
and love myself first
to end the cycle of seeking
from an outside source

And so, it goes much deeper
and holds more power
as I gently give rise
to this goddess inside

Who chalked up her worth
to another's kindness,
not knowing she was worthy
of love, blessings, abundance
all those things a father's love teaches

Last night I had a dream:
my best friend's dad hugged me,
grasping tightly as if to fill that
father wound from ages ago

Yet, I casually let go,
knowing it wasn't needed
as a long-awaited smile deployed
I finally filled the long-held void.

Swerve

When the voice of your parents when you were young
becomes your inner voice now grown,
when you realize it isn't yours,
it's up to you whether that voice endures,
keep the same path that's been sowed... or swerve?
letting old limitations turn to dust in the road.

We Aren't Alike

All my life I gave and gave
poured my heart down the drain,
despite being treated poorly,
I felt guilty for not giving you more

The choices I made weren't what was best for me
yet what was for you, though grown,
I played the familial role
just as I was expected to

You had each other, I was alone—
grief and loneliness added to my load
to now uncover, so I took on your patriarchal pain
because I couldn't stand to see you suffer,

You had less and I had more,
I shove it down and close the drawer,
I can't carry all of this, the body transforms
emerging as illness I couldn't solve,

Now you think I'm a hypochondriac
because I don't look sick at all
but you don't know how I feel,
still, I stay small

I tell you my body aches
you roll your eyes and call
me names behind my back,
not believing my pain until the surgeon
hands you the proof to unpack

Whisper down the lane
it all gets back to me,
never even an apology
pure betrayal to a tee,

I continue to accept your
flaws and trust you because
you smile and say you love me

My heart is screaming
watching me blindly trust and
accept you, when you never did me,
your forefather's pattern
repeating in various degrees

Fake smiles, conditional love,
nothing I could have done
that you didn't hold against me, your mistake

My love, my time, my compassion
all to you, I was the child, the glue
holding that falling-apart family together

Seeing clearly how one-sided it was
no matter how many years back I go,
I never received anything
nurturing, authentic, or true

Seeing my pattern unwind
not living in my power, it's time,
filtering out what isn't me, what isn't aligned
the child in me finally acknowledged and recognized
my eyes widen—we aren't wired the same,

My heart is pure love
I am filled with light,
while we have the same blood
we aren't alike

I'm the outsider who didn't belong—
the ugly duckling that was really a swan.

Burnt Popcorn

We stayed up all night
toasted strawberry pop tarts
the television to ourselves
laughing over the stench
of burnt popcorn
too many bags to count

So long as we were asleep
before our father's 4am alarm
tightly wound all day—
at night the watchman slept
no rules, no criticisms,
no tiptoeing around
the ticking time bomb,
the only feeling of freedom we got

The original TV bingers
flipping our seven channels late-night
resorting to all the movies on tape
for there was no cable in this regime,
forcing my eyes open obligingly
each time they tried to close,
making the most of
our late-night sovereignty

To the back patio
over sleeping dogs
set to a different clock
holding my breath as
I crack the fickle door,
carefully trying to ensure
it won't squeak as we slip out

The cool air meets our faces
watching clouds of smoke,
cicadas clicked, frogs croaked
the summer sky lit with fireflies
we laughed and talked and planned
our futures, our pranks
all was well, all was right
we were content in the
freedom of night

By ten to four
we'd sneak upstairs
trailing the burnt popcorn
as the smell filled the air
smiling to ourselves
before starting a full day's sleep

When the watchman rose before the sun
he was met with the obnoxious scent
of burnt popcorn and his own discontent.

Nothing into Something

You always had a name for me
dramatic, flighty, moody;
I heard it so much I started to believe it as truth
why did I have all these character flaws?
why weren't you proud of me just because?

You always knew better, so I gave away my power
wondering what was wrong with me,
why do I feel so unworthy?

Your relentless control went
beyond doing "what was best,"
as you so often disguised,
your love of logic spilled
into calculating manipulations

You plotted on, all your toxic traits
covered in shiny paper and fancy words
so no one caught on

You crossed all the lines
they weren't fine,
more like a gaping pothole,
that you had to jump across
and look me in the eye,
still, you didn't fold

You built me up with your words
and then broke me down behind closed doors,
your voice bellowed through,
a tantrum too big for someone so grown

My eyes filled with tears,
my body brimming with terror and fear,
all I can remember wrapped up
in an old pocketed sweater,
its warmth nurturing me
until I could leave,
the storm of you growled and stomped,
instigated, fueled the fire
Jekyll or Hyde? who am I getting today?

grown in that moment, taken back
by the emotional attack
my inner child in flight,
not knowing if you loved me or hated me
ultimately awakening me

A man whose earthly role is to
love and protect his offspring,
but you broke me into nothing
as you held this image of me
that wasn't true and you carried
more demons than you ever knew

I knew you couldn't love me
in the way I deserved, but I stayed—
that's what the indoctrination
taught me back when I was young,
knee-high socks, plaid skirts,
commandments, cultural norms,
molded into the good girl, the people pleaser,
hiding who I was to be who you wanted…
but where was the education on honoring myself,
on boundaries, on using my voice, on changing norms
that didn't make sense, on staying true to myself

I stayed so you could see the younger grow
my heart bigger than you'll ever know
instead, you told your tall tales,
smearing my name, scarring my heart
leaving me scraping and scrambling
only to wonder why you held my worth?

Deep in the negative numbers
I had much farther to rise,
much harder to teach myself
I am worthy, I am enough,
how one person's love, no matter his role,
has nothing to do with who I am

Humans playing their role
in this lifetime, as we take our lessons

for what they're worth and mine?
loving myself when no one else would

To all of those who grew without love,
look how far we've come, look how much
love we have to give; we always did,
time to give more of that to ourselves,

Letting it accumulate
a rose-gold fountain to wade in
any time we're taken back
to the moments of the past,
maybe we don't need to go again

One last visit

One last retell

One last cry over the old story
before its final farewell

I don't need to replay
I am safe
I am safe
to let the record retire
as my frequency rises
clearing space for new songs to play gently
remembering how loved I am
and how much more it means
because it started with me.

Hanging Up

I always said I love you before hanging up
waiting in stillness for you to say it back,
when I heard the click, I wondered if you heard me
my soft-spoken voice easily missed, *next time I'll speak louder
we all know your hearing goes as you get older*

Later came and as the conversation closed,
I spoke louder and clearer—only to hear the dial tone
wondering what I did to not earn your love

The pattern, the cycle, I was stuck in, I gave you
my worth to toss around but it was never yours to start,
your manipulating games, a counterexample of love,
the only thing you gave

Off to hug my inner child for putting up with you for too long
for letting you distort my views of love
for thinking I had to earn without condition,
something everyone deserves,
for living in the shadows
not realizing who I was

The horizon holding space for forgiveness
not only toward you, yet forgiving myself
for letting you to treat me as you did
as I hung onto every word, to your approval,
as if you were God

I won't be hanging on the phone anymore
the conversations ran their course
I'll never put my worth
into the hands of another—
it wasn't yours to have,
but it is mine to fix.

The Voice I Have Now

Apple juice across the floor,
walls scribbled with red and blue crayon,
playdough smushed into the rug—blame on
shaming, voice-raising,
criticisms outweighing
the compliments that didn't exist

Smiley face upside down,
unless the toys were away,
the report cards straight As
and we listened to every word you say

If I could go back, I'd spill the juice again,
without taking on your shaming,
I'd take the blame for the crayoned walls
the playdough-hardened carpet
to save my sibling from your degrading

I'd leave the dishes and laundry
and cups without coasters, and when you try
to make me feel worthless over what's undone,
I'd let it roll off my shoulders

But what will I not do?
I won't take your voice with me

The one telling me I wasn't good enough,
criticizing everything I was, making me feel
broken, unloved, worthless

You may have taught me to be polite,
to write my thank you notes,
to pay back every dollar owed
but love was never shown

The voice I have now is one I found
deep within the darkest corners of myself
digging to find what others held as a birthright

My inner voice will no longer be yours
the welcome mat's gone from the door,
no room for your lies obscured
years lost loving myself on your conditions—gone,
out the swinging door of the
brick house that looked like yours

My inner voice is one of love learned, not acquired,
feeling the depths of the nothingness you gave
the best counterexample I could ever receive
because my love, my heart, shines so bright
that even someone like you could feel my light

The love I have to give because of the lack I received
is more than I could ever imagine—
my heart in a wild expansion
as I can finally replace your voice with mine

Unearthed from brokenness, a newfound treasure trove
after feeling I was never enough to receive your love,
I can finally feel my own.

Words to the Wind

In a fit of fury
I threw down a boundary—
a tarp covering the ground beside my door
an unwelcome mat of sorts,
yet nothing to hold the corners,
nothing to keep it in place,
swept by a single gust,
off it went with the wind's breath.

The Puppeteer

Don't be a burden, don't be thirsty, don't touch anything,
not even the railing, be better behaved than all the rest,
get the most compliments—all a show,
when the curtain was drawn
a different story awaited than the play
you carefully orchestrated

I didn't touch a thing, I didn't respond yes
when asked if I wanted a drink, as others dug
through cabinets, smearing handprints across the glass,
being children, as I stood still, quiet,
voiceless—a doll in the corner

When I used my voice for thoughts buzzing around my head,
like why different religions instead of just one—
shut down by your shrill outbursts,
zero to one hundred over spilled juice,
your inflamed voice, explosive behavior,
the way you blamed, degraded, and shamed,
I kept turning my volume down,
filtering what I should and shouldn't say
overthinking, analyzing what wouldn't be met
with a tantrum today

Until I stopped speaking, quiet and still,
I followed your programming
doing the things that earned me praise,
trained like Pavlov's dog under your control,
I cleaned, organized, and took care of the younger
but I didn't use my voice any longer

I fell into the role of the good girl,
no opinions, no speaking up, yes sir,
blindly following your command
manipulation out of hand

Once you fall into a role to keep you safe
it's that much harder to have a voice again,
every time you speak replaying in your head
wondering if it sounded okay
waiting for the validating,
so you can breathe again

Now I see ever so clearly
you tried to silence me
your toxic masculinity,
narcissistic undertones bellowing over
using force to make me feel weak,
worthless, and unimportant

Your towering presence filled the room—
a tyrannosaurus rex standing over his prey,
but my arms are long and they can reach,
I have the ability to stretch,
to know when I'm being pushed out
to know when it's time to find my strength,
no longer will your dark shadow crawl
across the floor, nipping at my toes
as I sit oblivious
not anymore

You raised me to feel unloved and unvalued,
I had no choice but to stay the course,
yet I did as I matured, by then your reach,
your grasp too strong for me to break,
you chipped away so many pieces of me
I wasn't whole enough to walk away

I should've left that baseball game
when you spilled beer on the mascot,
heckling him for an accidental bump
the crowd destroyed you,
and I took your side

I should've left each time
I spoke my mind, my brilliant mind,
and it was met with a pound on the table,
a belt on the chair, the rage across your face
over a comment you disagreed with

I should've left when you arrived
to my matrimony only to walk out,
the look of disgrace across your face,
I didn't know I deserved better than you,
the irony lost

I should've left when he departed
due to the unsafe space you created
and he blamed himself—pure manipulation,
somehow I was strong enough to survive
not without his help earthside

I should've left when your whispers
reached me at the end of the lane
all times you spoke my name
out of the context of goodness,
for which I am

I want to say that I walked away from you
with my head held high, in my power all the time,
but it was more like a crawl across the floor under a
sleeping grizzly, scampering to the snores, trying to not be seen
so I could safely escape and figure out who I was again

Never will I let toxic masculinity touch me again
never will I bow my head to those who tower over me,

I will find my voice again, and I will turn up the volume,
I will connect without fear, I will learn how to stand
in my power this time around,
without the puppeteer.

Not There Yet

Am I at forgiveness?

No, not yet

Am I stuck in victimhood?

No, not quite

In this place of in-between,
where the hurt runs
deep as the river,

Water is always moving
carving new landscapes,
emptying and creating all the same
in the river's gaze,

I spend time in stillness
feeling and freeing
the cascade;
pain, hurt, betrayal
flow away in waves,
with great power to shape,

As I feel and free past emotion
my terrain starts to change,
my body made of water
not so different from the river,

And that's when the connection rings out:
emptying and creating are not so far apart.

From Where I Stood

Blurred faces, hands shaking, eyes down,
so they won't meet the sadness all around,
I let the tears flow freely as I spoke

You, stoic and strong with dry eyes and even at times,
a smile, I was in awe of how you held yourself
together in that heart-wrenching moment
as I tore through the tissue box,
I couldn't wrap my mind around
how you were able to pull together,
how you could have such strength
when I was a weeping mess,

Your banter and praise of how I kept the day
moving as others were too broken,
and that's how I fell into the role of the fixer

Now with my grown eyes, I see I was a child,
overwhelmed by large emotions,
and when I needed an example, a role model,
someone to show me how to process,
you stood tall, cold, tearless like nothing happened,
as you stuffed and stumbled and suppressed
every feeling you ever had—even the good ones,

I was so focused on my loss
I wanted to keep what I had left,
I held you on that pedestal
looking up from down below

Trying to control my emotion
so I could be just like you,
ignoring the signs from my body,
as it tried to show me how to handle
tough feelings, wanting to send them packing
just as you sent yours,
holding them in for years and years
into illness, they turned and the roles I picked up—
the fixer, the good girl, the glue,
no longer served

When I step to the right,
when I clean the dirt and debris off the lens,
change the focus, zoom out, take in, let the ground even,
I find nothing looks the same as it did,
from where I first stood

Over here is not the same as over there
strong and stoic you were not,
living in the disconnect,
handed down to me—
mine to work through with intent

Returning to the day I stopped the tears
and sitting with myself,
giving her so much love
while she lets them fall again,
letting the intensities come up
instead of staying stuck,
I tell her it all works out beautifully
better than she could even dream
yet this was part of her path
to take lessons and move past

She has the strength to show up
for herself, not to fix or solve,
she knows to honor herself,
connect to her heart,
let her intuition guide her,
not others, no earthly being,
no matter their label this lifetime

Where I stood
is not where I stand now
the footprints down a different path,
no longer trying to fill,
feelings flowing as designed
a beautiful trail of—
scattered leaves
and love.

Return to Strangers

That time I waved you on at the gas station
as you tried to pull into an endless string of cars
I waved you on, then saw it was you,
but you didn't see me

You gave such a grateful wave as if to tip your hat
in an old Southern charmer sort of way,
what a kind man you looked to be,
strange, you never gave that kindness to me
that time I waved you on at the gas station

We were thirty minutes from both our homes
I, driving home from a masters class,
you, going out of your way for the cheapest gas
I saw you, but you didn't see me

Minutes from your childhood home,
the one you couldn't move on from,
circling your past instead of creating better
I quietly remember that time I waved you on at the gas station

The Sunoco sign takes me straight back
you'd say "Fill-er up with Plus" in a voice so counterfeit
I'd wonder how others believed, rolling my eyes as I watched the
numbers rise from the backseat of the station wagon

You'd quickly crank up the window
barely making it up before you found a reason to unload
the very pattern that broke you was the one you kept fueling
that time I waved you on at the gas station

Watching a man ball up his receipt, I recall
how you kept yours neatly piled in the console
a running tab on everything under your control
I saw you, but you didn't see me

That night, that cheerful smile, that thankful wave,
that might've been the nicest you ever were to me
you never really knew me, or maybe I never felt
I could show you who I really was
that time I waved you on at the gas station
I knew you like the back of my hand
years I spent watching your behavior trying not to set you off
years I spent following your command, as I was dragged along
I saw you, I always saw you, but you didn't see me

I'd try to have my voice heard, but it was always
met with tantrums so big for someone so grown—
a constant balancing of your emotions with mine
so much that I lost myself in the unknown
until I had to say goodbye
but you had called it quits on me long before

That time I waved you on at the gas station
and you didn't know it was me, might have been
the only time you looked at me favorably

And that's how we'll leave it,
a simple reset, a hop on the timeline,
two strangers letting their earthly
roles fall to the side

That time I waved you on at the gas station
I saw you, I always saw you
but you never truly saw me.

In-Between

I thought you were everything,
when really I stayed small
shrinking myself to nothing in your company
seeking your approval, buying into your schemes
led to believe you knew more than me

I knew you weren't the greatest, no role model of mine,
still, your hold ran as deep as the sands of time
each time I stepped out to make choices and a life,
pulled right back into your grasp
tiptoeing around, trying to please, balancing you and me,
when there was *only me*

I couldn't be everything you wanted me to be,
I couldn't be everything I knew I was,
and so, I landed in the in-between

The in-between doesn't serve anyone,
it certainly won't please you, as nothing will,
it certainly won't please me as I'm not living authentically,
holding onto the notion that you would finally see me
and understand how amazing I am, but that's the same thinking
that landed me in the in-between

I can't people-please my life away
regardless of your label or your role—
it's not why I'm here
if you don't see how bright I shine,
that's on you

I stand in my power, my truth
open my eyes and face what I always knew,
letting your hold fall away and transmute,
as I stand tall and strong as me
not the in-between, authentically aligned

with the depths of my soul,
stepping out fully and completely
knowing and trusting
what's best for me

And if I fall back,
wondering who I am,
if I'm in the in-between again
I can simply ask myself,

Is this aligned with me?
breathing fresh air in,
new paths open, life in my eyes
as the old versions,
the in-between gently subsides.

The Storm of You

A love that should've
protected me, sheltered me—*shattered* me,
crushed seashells in the sand, all the pieces of me strewn across the beach,
it would take an eternity to collect and piece together— and so,
I let go of my brokenness, and start again,
remnants of who I was wash away,
all but one—pearl-white, ridged,
wing-shaped, to remind me
that angels will hold me,
until I can rise
again

Long Before

I would have loved you forever,
until the stars ceased to sparkle,
compassion and loyalty
knocked me to my knees
a different view than before,
the day everything changed

I would have loved you forever
a promise I made to myself
for you to no longer suffer
any more than you had

I would be the fixer, the glue,
the voice of reason, I would carry
all the things no one could
I would take on the weight of the world
for what I thought was love

I would have loved you forever
my heart, tender and pure
thinking mine was born from yours,
yet we aren't designed the same,
my rose-gold fountain fills me up
while you feed on what isn't yours,
our feet may walk the same earth,
our hearts on different planes

I would have loved you forever
that's just who I am,
until I spun around
and the mountains fell, crashing into the ground
the world inverted I had no idea
as I had faced the other way for so long

As I start to really see, my eyes strain
aching from what's now in front of me—
a long-carried blind spot,
compliments tossed to throw me off,
confusing them for goodness— the filter now off

I would have loved you forever
but I had to choose myself
we are not the same—
the love I never felt from you
the love I always held
the love I give mine
the love I need to give myself
to start again

I would have loved you forever
until the stars ceased to sparkle
yet you let me go long before,
it took me thousands of days to see
with heart-breaking clarity.

Someone I Knew

With a smile, you'd give
someone the shirt off your back
only to turn around,

To spend ten long years
miserably complaining
that they took your clothes.

Through My Dreams, I Heal

Last night I dreamt
I wrote all I'd been through,
in a letter from deep within
written to two with a likeness to me,
but it wasn't meant for you

My words were not received
they turned their backs,
their noses high in the air,
Anastasia and Drizella,
as you watched,
I saw your eyes soften

I don't know if you read my words
or maybe you just knew
and defended me from the unkind two
while their minds weren't changed,
I felt seen by you in a way I never have before

While you and I will never
in this lifetime see eye-to-eye
our higher selves connected,
in a dreamy stance
letting our souls heal
from the trauma within

I wake in awe
of you, of me,
and this beautiful gift:
healing dreams
to restore.

Lower the Pedestal

When someone fills a role meant for a mother, father, or sibling, it feels so incredible to have love in that space that you can easily sensationalize, so you no longer see them as they are—
but what they did for you

The someone who momentarily filled that role is just a person, like you, let the attachment go, you are whole and complete just the way you are, even if no one ever told you that

That love and kindness the person gave was given freely, without debt, they wanted to give, and you were open to receive

Honor their kindness, know you are worthy of blessings and abundance, but don't make someone else the hero in your story

No matter how much their kindness meant,
No matter how loved you felt,

You're the hero in your story.

Passing You

I can finally pass you in a restaurant
and smile and nod
as you sip your soup
across the room
I can wait to be seated,
without feeling all the feelings
as I already have

Though some might flow
through now and again
as I find my footing, my balance,
I tiptoe around the softness
of forgiveness after being served
raw anguish

You and I
have always been complicated
I'm the change-maker
the break in the generational line
something I had in me all the time,
the volcano that thought it was a mountain,
until the magma rose destructing what was
for the betterment of all

I cried for thousands of days
as I cleaned up the debris
and tried to move on, but I never forgave
the list too long, the pain too deep
hard to wrap my tender heart around

Until, I reframed
working through the erupted emotions
accepting what was,
what is, what could be,
we all have roles in this earthly land
that guide us through the lessons
we came to learn

Betrayal and pain is what I received
but now I have a choice—
to dwell, to rehash, to stew,
or to feel, accept, and grow,
finding the hidden gifts,
letting forgiveness
softly land between us

Forgiveness is *not* okaying your actions
rather freeing myself from the feelings I held
as part of my expansion,

I forgive you for me—
to free myself of your hold
for my own healing, my soul's growth,
yet that doesn't mean
I let you back in

I'll nod from over here
knowing I'm not harboring the past
within me anymore

Seeing you again doesn't feel
like I've been hit by a tidal wave
as it once did, but rather,
lukewarm waters soaking my toes
showing me I can move forward

Letting the old wash away
in the waves of yesterday.

Greatness

You had confidence in who you were,
a type of power I couldn't quite match,
where you were up high and I was down low

I went through my life like that,
thinking all others as higher than myself
until someone treated me as I was

Then, instead of realizing that greatness was within me too,
I idolized the person who finally saw greatness within me

When will we realize we are not outside of ourselves,
we are greatness, we are love, just by default
and no one can tell us we are not,
you are no different than me
though I spent my days thinking differently

A script running in my head making me a character
you omniscient, fan fiction at play,
seeking the validation I never received
looking outside of myself to feel complete,
but if it's just me and these words
the wholeness must come from within first

I am greatness, I am love, I will radiate out
releasing the days I was in doubt,
I was taught backward and had to spin
to find my way out.

Gently Looking Back

I distinctly remember
there was goodness and laughter
and memories to smile back on

By now, you've picked it all apart,
nothing I ever could say or do
would change that

Somehow we can look
at the same thing and see differently,
you and I don't have the same capacity

Deep down I know
there won't be a day where you
remember my actions, my heart, myself
with the love I deserve

Yet, I can hold these reveries with love
that's what I'm made of, as are you,
if you lift the fog that surrounds

When I gently look back
I am able to look with love,
and I'm grateful for that.

Reset

Pulling the string to turn on the light
I settle in the old dusty armchair—
this corner of my mind
I pushed so far to the side

Sinking into the memories
letting them come forward,
now that I have the capacity
to reflect from a place of neutrality

Not one of anger, not one of hate,
not one of dwelling in shame
but sitting with an open heart thinking
over the deflated struggles of yesterday

I wait for the towering emotion
that used to overtake, but none awakes
I can look back and see with clarity,
roles played, boundaries muddled, heartache,
blind spots, lessons learned, as I move forward

A graduation of some sort, prouder than any diploma
for this one surpasses—echoes of soul expansion

The ability to work through charged experiences
and set them back to neutral,
free of the clutter that used to take up space
not a speck of dust remains,
shadows gone, stories away
nothing left to do in this place

Pulling the string to turn off the light.

One Last Thing

When I was young, you told me
I could say everything I wanted to say
but with a kinder voice,
though you didn't take your own advice
not even once—
but I did, maybe that could be
the one thing you taught me.

3

Breaking Previous Patterns

*It's ready to leave
when you're ready to let go—
you decide it's time.*

Rebuilding

When you build a house in the sand
and wonder why it's slanted

When you chase practical dreams
and run out of breath

When you spend life looking good on paper
but don't recognize yourself in the mirror

When you do the same thing over and over
and expect a different outcome

There's a part of you that breaks
no matter how many boxes you've checked,
your heart isn't content

This isn't how you saw yourself, your dreams were greater
where is the person who defied all odds that awaited?

You can blame others, the circumstance,
wade in limiting beliefs and doubt, thinking you're not
good enough or things never work out

That's normally where we get stuck
for years and years, the same cycle
letting the world drain us of the vibrance we once had

But maybe, just maybe, you were meant for bigger things,
not to settle in the in-between

You realize there's different work to be done
digging deeper, realigning, filling your cup
surrendering to the fall and rebuilding
from the ground up.

Broken Clock

I used to chase time
wondering where it all went,
illusion at best.

Shifting

How do you shift an old belief system
when it's a part of who you are?

You think it's keeping you safe,
but it's keeping you small.

Another box to break free from, but how?

This Again

When I turn corner after corner
only to end up in what feels like the same place

I want to wallow in gloom, pity, disarray
but there's a choice to be made
to repeat, or to break the cycle

Maybe I'm back where I was
so I can make a different choice

Maybe I'm back where I was
as a grand finale to all the pain

Because this time,
I have the tools, the strength
to rise through.

Alchemy

Such a strange life we are in
where those we walk alongside
who are *supposed* to love and support us,
trigger us

In these moments,
feeling bothered, broken, confused
how can we be spiritual beings
and feel so out of tune?

We can turn our heads and say,
they're trying their best,
we can try to be the bigger person and just ignore,
we can pretend we didn't feel so distressed when really,
this is how the earthly plane is *meant* to feel,

The people we love will trigger us
as part of our soul's growth,
part theirs, part ours
the unspoken law of the land:
we're here to learn
to check off the boxes,
not the chores, not the errands,
but the lessons of our time,
each unique to our soul's many lifetimes
since we can't fix something we can't see,
things that feel like a setback
are meant to push us to dig deep

Emotions we collect can be released
like a beautiful geyser,
or build and erupt like Mount Vesuvius,
whether we work through our triggers or repeat
is our choice

Already walking through the mud
why not find our way out,
instead of staying stuck,
surrendering to the learning,
sinking into the feeling,
letting go of the inner child's beliefs
where that trigger probably came from,

Maybe setting a boundary, maybe creating space,
maybe quieting the ego so hearts can speak

Aligning our throat,
one step up, one step down,
with our heart, our third eye
clearing, balancing, equalizing
wrapping it all in love,
and using our true voice,
taking the lessons and shifting
into a being of pure magic

You are the alchemist—
the alchemist of your time
that can take any challenge and turn it to gold,
not walk away, not let your ego get caught in roles,
not getting locked into the same cycles,
letting your heart guide you
as you quiet your mind

The people who are *supposed* to love us do,
that's why they signed up to guide you
and you them, a divine act of love,

There are no mistakes, each experience unique,
the answer is in you when you connect—
all paths intertwine
with one beautiful goal in mind:
your soul's growth in this lifetime

And once we're out of the mud,
our feet can be cleaned
fresh and light, boxes checked
until the next trigger comes along,
we've already eased out once

So long as you remember, there's nothing wrong with you,
there's nothing wrong with the feelings that arise,
you are loved each and every day
whether you feel it or not,
yet, you don't need to carry the old stories
slung across your back
once you put them down, your lens will clear,
and you can see the opportunity to go from there

Knowing you are loved
you are supported by those on earth and those above,
and when you change the filter and really see,
this land isn't such a strange place to be

It all comes together beautifully,
you're here to learn and grow—
support is there each time you connect,

You have power to shift
you are the alchemist.

Cycle-Breaker

Do you ever feel stuck in the same old patterns,
wishing you can change?

If you run before you grow, it's a temporary fix
because you'll just repeat, until you break
the patterns that run deep,
freeing yourself from the cycle of yourself,
that's not really you,

You are not your pattern,
you are not even your feelings

You are not what happened to you,
that almost broke but didn't
cause your strength pulled you through,

You are a divine being of embers once ignited,
glowing stardust,
the wind's breath,
the ocean herself

The elements that surround you,
are in you, are you,

Yet the mind leads us astray
causing feelings of separation when
you are one with the Trees,
the Waters, the Grasses, the Mountains

They send their wind-blown messages to you
waiting for you to notice,
how well they know you,
how well they know your family line,
seeing the patterns and cycles accrue,

You're the bearer of change,
the one they've waited for
to acknowledge what needed to break,
here for support, for remembrance, for magic
you can create the waves,
the change you want, deep within
and it will radiate,
the sun beaming through the forest
bringing light to where it was dark
your ancestors joyfully cheer
through the frequency of birds,
flocks gathered together to remind,
you are supported with love and light
for how could you not?

You are a divine being,
woven by the Creator who made the sun,
the stars,
the wind,
the mountains,
the waters,
and you,

Within your heart is the strength,
the support, the knowledge
to end the cycle and start anew

They're waiting, you're waiting,
as your power surmounts
into the change you so greatly want.

From the Wind

That time the wind wept, I wept too
I wept in sadness, in grief, in loss
I wept for all I went through,
but I learned a lifetime of lessons
from the howling wind that night—

To let the negative emotions flow out
instead of keeping them disguised,
that I can suppress them all I want
but there's no camouflage the body can hide—

Each emotion should be felt and honored
not just the ones that bring joy,
there's a whole prism of other feelings
that are waiting for healing—

It's okay to *feel* even if I wasn't shown how,
it's alright to be the walking waterfall,
it doesn't make me fragile rather shows my strength
there's not a single soul that would describe the wind as weak

I know its power, just as I know mine and yours,
but if I keep everything in, there's going to be a time it storms,
and when it arrives, I have a choice—

Embrace what comes, watch all I've held wash away
and let myself heal in the disarray—
or I can stay the same,
my decision to make

This life we live in human form
brings pain and sadness as part of our growth,
and while we can try to cover those
with a cheerful face, a smile, a bow,
they're still there unless we consciously let go

We can move on without the things we've held
we can create new patterns around feelings
we are our own healers

That time the wind wept, I wept too
I wept in sadness, in grief, in loss,
feeling and freeing all I went through
the wind made it okay for me to breakdown too.

Scribbles

How do you break a pattern scribbled
on yourself when you were young?

Childhood scaffolds in place to keep you safe,
you grow and change, unknowingly carrying the past
like a pocket stone you didn't know you held

Rethinking relationships, self-worth, self-love,
you find lifelong patterns that kept you safe now need to break,
returning to your inner child with the broken crayons,
turning those scribbles into a piece of art

Your journey now more beautiful than you could have imagined,
beneath those scribbles was a girl worthy of love
as she was, this artwork is a reminder if she falls back,
as we are not perfect, just learners along this path.

Backlog

There's enough suppressed emotion
to flood the river banks if it all came out at once
and so it trickles, wreaking havoc along the way,
wondering what is going to come up today

One moment fine and not the next,
neighborhoods changing in the blink of an eye
looking for a way out, eyes on the road
but the only way out is through

Past the mess, the fogginess, the tear-stained eyes,
the things that scare us most,
wondering if we'll get to the other side
praying our vessel keeps moving
and doesn't breakdown

And so, my prayers change
instead of asking for help out,
I ask for help through, otherwise,
nothing changes, this I know

How can I show up for myself today?
How can I listen to my body in new ways?
How can I open my mind and heart
to receive the goodness that comes in?
How can I honor my inner child,
and the things she's still carrying?

My heart a cluttered office,
papers stacked to the ceiling
closet stuffed so the door won't shut
I can make a fresh start, I can create new habits,
yet I still have to sort the backlog created,
decluttering all I accumulated
working on the stockpile I've suppressed,

now turned to symptoms,
I won't will them away or place a band-aid,
but sift through the stacks, little by little each day

And as I do
a message comes through—
I'm capable of changing this trajectory,
just like all the others I've transformed,
the rainbow road leading out
so many patterns and places have fallen away

Where you feel stuck
remember your strength in all those times,
you showed up for yourself,
you had divine support,
you were able to ascend higher
than you thought you could

This is no different,
a long, deep-rooted pattern,
from before you could comprehend,
the arduous landscaping rock
that couldn't be moved,
but it was—with strength and tools and patience
and time in part, a new garden grew in that spot

Let the pattern fall away as you rise
you have this in you, closer than you think,
not even arm's reach away
you are capable of this and more,
tune in to yourself
let the old cycles soften and dissolve,
uncaging what you gripped,
feeling, freeing, believing
and leaning into the shift.

Mirrored Water

Thousands and thousands of years old
water carrying memory
no longer flowing
puddled to stagnancy
mold growing
inside these four walls
black dots across the ceiling
only the beginning
running into it over and over and over again
not learning my lesson
that I have internalized so much emotion
it has turned stagnant inside of me
causing sickness and symptoms
that the mold I keep running into
is a mirror of what I'm holding
in my body.

Yellowed Pages

I am learning to feel emotion, instead of keeping it
like an old scrapbook that's no longer relevant,
worn, yellowed papers stuck together like sap on the tree,
roots going deep, filled to the brim with every emotion
I never let go of, but the tree doesn't fall,
she gets stronger and taller and more balanced,
her muscle memory doesn't weaken, but
at some point, she has to be releasing
all the stuck emotions,
the energy should be in motion,
it's not as easy as tossing them
or wiping the pages clean,
first to open the flow
so the emotion can cycle out,
the backlog from decades and decades ago,
taking time to go through the old scrapbook
and acknowledge and release,
and thank, and clear the space.

Letting Go

That thing
you are still grieving
was never for you—
it was a diving board
that felt like a ditch,
you thought you were trying to climb out
but really you were learning to swim

In waters you've never been before
but always dreamt of,
maybe not this lifetime
but your soul carried the dream,

Holding it like a heart-shaped locket
until you remember,
it's time to open it up
and live how you
were meant.

Softening

I can let my fear soften
letting its opacity lighten,
dissolving, dissipating
as I step into all the goodness
that fear kept me from.

Crosswalk

She walked along the road careful not to step on cracks, eye over her shoulder, every slight movement, keenly aware of every possible thing that could go astray, even in the safest of places.

She preferred looking back at her travel photos, all the places she had been, rather than actually being there, as she knew she was safe and sound again.

Always playing it safe, she didn't take risks or engage in any adventures or games— nor put herself in any situation that made her uncomfortable.

Cautious she called it. *I'm just cautious*. Yet, she carried so much trauma, which surfaced in fear, causing her to let life pass her by while she cried, wondering what was wrong with her.

She wasn't really living, missing all the beauty, losing joy in worry.

It took unlearning, unwinding, returning to her body, her breath, letting her heart, her intuition feel what she needed to— rather than her mind spin out. She put words to what she was really scared of. She faced fear, it took courage. She found strength.

A lot of what she carried didn't belong to her, some from other generations, lifetimes, conditioning.

However, it was hers to let go of.

Now she walks along the cracks, her body feeling lighter, not giving heed to the fear that once leashed her. She feels safety and freedom simultaneously within herself.

And she might fall back, but she has the ability this time to move forward again.

Goodbye Fear

And just like that, the clouds clear
and I connect with my intuition,
knowing this moment of worry
is part of my humanness and doesn't define my soul

My connection to my divinity brings me peace,
the peace I've searched my whole life for—
I tried to receive it by pleasing others,
piling on accomplishments, milestones,
tallying it all up, for nothing in return

Clearing out the trauma, the things that didn't belong to me
but felt like they were me, as I gave them a home
for as long as I can remember

If I go way back, I recall when fear wasn't a part of me,
when I played in the dark rooms
everyone else was afraid to go,
when a bat flew into our house and my father hid
but I went looking (it was a bird by the way),
when my best friend was a dog
twice as big as me

There was a time when fear didn't dominate my body
when fear didn't cloud my decisions
when fear didn't pop out at every moment of disarray

This moment of peace brings me back,
this glimmer of hope, this break in the clouds
for one moment reminds me of who I am
and who I'm not

There was a time before fear,
and soon, they'll be an after.

Present

The pain comes
when I think of the past,
I get stuck in a loop—
what I would change,
what I should have said,
justifying my feelings,
and I realize I'm stuck
in my head

The worry comes
when I think of the future—
what could happen,
the past repeating,
fretting over different scenarios,
I desperately want to know
that everything will be okay

The peace comes
when I'm in the present,
really and truly in this moment,
here, now, all is well

As I hold space
in the here and now,
the illusion of time passes without note,
the future becomes the present
and everything is still okay.

Innermost

You can soften your responses
to drop out of the patterns you carried
that kept you safe for so long

You can soften and drop in
to your heart to speak
from a place of love

Going deeper
than surface vocals
all clogged

Just as the violinist
tunes his strings each time he plays,
our voice is the instrument of our soul

Channeled through our roots,
our sacral, our solar plexus,
our heart, our third eye,
our crown
our voice is sacred

And if we don't clear and calibrate
ourselves to the frequency of love,
then what comes out?

Emotions, experiences,
they get the best of us—
obstructing our true voice
with fear, guilt, shame, limiting beliefs,
breaches of power, weak boundaries,
and other energies that don't belong

As your voice
connects to what is greater
it will clear surface-level debris,
no longer you, never was,
letting it dissipate gently
until it's gone

Deepen and soften,
reconnecting your voice,
to your innermost self,
stronger than it's ever been

So that each time you speak,
it comes from deep within,
rooted from a space of love

That's what you are,
that's what you bring

Let your voice be your mirror—
listen to really hear her

When she comes to the surface
a divine miracle in itself,
root her in love.

Not Who I Was

I am the snake
shedding old versions of myself,
slowly transforming into everything
I've always known.

Voiceless

My voice was soft and sweet like honey, so high-pitched
it was almost counterfeit, I couldn't let my true words out,
it wasn't safe to be me

I lost myself so easily, saying what I was expected to say,
doing what I was expected to do, filling the roles
other people told me to, being everything for everyone else
that I, whoever that was, was a fraction
of who I was meant to be

Worn like an old slipper with a broken sole,
my voice became raspy, uneven, easily shaken
as my soul cried out to just notice—
to note the disconnect, to just be aware,
to wake up from the hibernation
that should have been a nap
I tried to remember how to take up space,
to stand tall, yet my voice would betray,
once again it cracked

The pendulum swung
from one side to the other, missing the balance
the lifetimes before where I had no voice, this was not that,
this was the lifetime for me to figure it out,
how to use my voice authentically
in balance, in love, in clarity,
to no longer people-please
or speak what others want me to say,
nor use my voice to hide myself
but to speak with love, and not sharp or harsh,
nothing of that in my heart

Turning to nature for its wisdom,
humming along with the birds to connect our frequencies
as they use their vocals in wondrous ways

connecting to my breath, letting it clear the pathways
breathing into all the parts of myself in disconnect

Knowing I cannot be everything and
no one is meant to be, putting boundaries in place
to honor myself and keep me safe,
not letting just anyone through,
repairing the broken-down shack I always knew
with walls upheld and a door that swings—
energetic boundaries

Honoring my inner child and all she went through,
how quieting her voice was a survival skill
but now she's grown, she is me,
and she can heal her carried trauma,
rewiring her nervous system to shake off the fear—
we are not walking on eggshells around here

Feeling old emotions surface, one-by-one ancient collector items
leave the rusty shelves, closing sale, everything must go—
my load lightens from all I held onto

Visualizing my heart with my voice,
with my divinity, all interlinked
as a trinity of purple, blue, and pink,
to use my voice as the miracle it is

Speaking my truth freely and openly with kindness and love,
but first listening to myself above all else
knowing I am aligned with my authenticity

Just like the mermaid in the sea,
whose voice returned after tragedy
the ultimate despair-to-triumph story,
where her voice returns in balance, in clarity.

I'm So Over You

Inviting me and tugging at my heart
holding us for years too short,
little signs you sent—
bunnies through the neighborhood,
fresh-baked cookies at the door,
showing this is where we were meant
to root, to rest, to explore

Never more than a dream I couldn't quite hold,
too slippery, too wiggly, the foundation cracked—
I sleep with one eye open, never fully relaxed,
trees lined the yard with their secret paths,
pink flowers I could see from my bath,
space we had dreamt about, water to help us flow
to nourish, to nurture, to bestow

Until the Christmas we never had,
teased with stockings and a seven-foot tree
we didn't sing a single song around, no parcels beneath,
a gift that wasn't ours to keep, the fixtures that never sat right
a layout I didn't like, the arguments flying
the stale air spreading, my heart was never one hundred

Attempted to decorate but it never came to be,
lights cast to the side for weeks
I rested but never really slept,
my mind always spinning out
but I'm not there anymore
we are out, and I'm so over you,

I'm so over you for finding me,
and reeling me in
and moving me to decisions
that never felt good,
you may be grateful to me
but I'm just plain sad,
and so,
very so,
over you.

Ancient History

Remember when traveling somewhere unfamiliar, you had to print out directions on MapQuest? And, if you missed your turn, you backtracked.

Remember when you had to dial into AOL to type to your friends? Hoping it connected, instead of leaving you stuck on the dial tone?

Remember when phones had cords, you needed a quarter to dial home?

Or, when you had to rewind a cassette tape to hear the same song again? Singing wrong words unless you were lucky enough to get lyrics on the insert.

Our technology has changed and evolved so much in such a short time. If everything around us changes, can't you see that we're meant to change also?

We can't stay stuck with the same patterns. Imagine if we still played music on cassettes—and never moved to what came next.

We weren't meant to live our life with a crumpled tape deck.

Nor were we meant to follow directions on a piece of printed paper.

Nor "text" our friends through a desktop computer.

If our old comforts are obsolete, what does that make our old patterns?

We think they're keeping us safe, but they're keeping us stuck in the past when there are better things waiting.

We are meant to grow, change, evolve. Let yourself. You aren't a wrinkled cassette from yesterday.

You are something even greater than what's already here.

The rest is ancient history.

Spiritual Math

Let's pull out the lessons
instead of the criticisms
instead of the nagging voice in your head—
you've done it again

Let's pull out the lessons
instead of wallowing in regret
instead of feeling less-than

You know it's all for a reason
you know you are an amazing being
you have a scroll of all the things
you signed up for, some of which are tough

Just for tonight, let's wade in forgiveness,
the rose-gold fountain of our goddess,
vase in hand she pours water,
cleansing, clearing, filling
until your heart is so full
that all you feel is love—your own love
and that is enough

You can calm and regulate your nervous system,
knowing it's all meant as it was,
but you can't keep repeating
the long-engrained pattern every time
your heart starts beating the way it did

Tap into divinity, a greater channel flowing in,
as it's always supporting you
knowing you are safe and whole,
the triggers are just the past returning—
an opportunity for you
to evolve and grow.

The Pause

When your pocket gets stuck on the drawer handle,
do you push yourself free,
or do you realize you're stuck and pause?
taking a moment to unhook
before going on your way?

Why do we forget the pause?
taking a moment, a breath, a break
not analyzing or victimizing or intellectualizing
but just giving yourself a pause
because when you do,
it's easier to unhook
and move
again.

Cutting Cords

I call in support,
breathe and release
freeing myself from those
that no longer serve

Yet there's more to be released,
what am I forgetting?

More cords to cut
freeing me from
old versions of myself.

Healing Hearts

You swooped in at a time I needed change
from so much that felt like failure—
failed father, late brother, broken heart
no masculine figure that still had a presence,
one hundred to zero the prominent pattern

Though I tried to push you away
you fluttered in, wings strong, always around
leaving trails of heart-shaped petals on stable ground

Your soft-spoken voice, your gentle way, your kindness,
you listened, I was heard, my ego wanted no part,
my heart wanted it all

Then we stopped trying—
I kept talking, you stopped listening,
my words got sharp, your warmth whittled away,
you triggered my childhood issues, and I yours,
as we reflected the low roads of each other

Looking through a mended lens,
seeing it for what it was, healing all that came before—
inner road work, clearing the debris, cracks in the concrete,
old patterns obsolete, if we have the strength
to shift into something greater,
our hearts can heal together.

Programming

It's hard work taking care of this mind, body,
and soul in a whole new way,

Slowly chipping away at old patterns
losing the charge, letting them fall to neutral
while creating new ones,

Figuring out how to clear away the dust
to find connection to your body without losing your way
through the sneezing,

Figuring out how to connect to your intuition
a feeling, a voice, a knowingness when before
that voice was only fear,

Reprogramming your mind to soften the fear, the worry,
endless loopholes of what could be and step into trust
and forgiveness, just because it happened before,
doesn't mean it will again, you are deserving of more,

Spending time in stillness and rest
when before you never stopped moving,
addicted to thoughtless tasks, marathons for your mind
to keep it occupied so you wouldn't fall out,
not knowing the opposite is what you needed,

Processing the grief, the sorrow, the pain, the moments
that you thought broke you, but you didn't break,
you stretched for higher, and pulled yourself up
but looking back is still tough,

Reframing all that happened before as part of your path,
part of your karmic lessons in this land, and all of
those difficult moments show your rise-up,
shedding away all that came before

Rewiring the body, the mind, the soul to work together,
a sacred trinity, instead of one running ahead,
while the others fall back, together in harmony
how it was meant to be, how we fell away
in this programmed society,

The program we thought we held
with all the details of the how play will go—
the stage, the acts, the intermission, the lighting, the crew
when you open the program up
it's empty—unwritten

There's nothing to let fall away,
except the story we carried in our mind,
but it takes time and patience
to get to this new place
so be gentle with yourself

You are here for the magic of the old falling away,
a new foundation being built,
as this migration to the age of love arrives

Your light is your anchor shining up the old parts,
finding what we need within ourselves
so our body, mind, and soul
work together, as meant to be

The fall was part of the rise,
the ash clearing the way
rewiring, brightening, strengthening,
letting yesterday's program
softly fall away.

Lanterns in the Sky

Just as the laughs, the stories,
the adages resurface from childhood,
so does the pain, trickling through
arriving in moments and blips
to be healed and sent off
like a Chinese lantern in the sky

Yet, you are harping on the pain,
triggers, turmoil because it's what you know,
you are comfortable in chaos because it's how you grew,
you are holding and hoarding the lanterns that are ready to go

It's hard work to break old patterns, to make new choices,
to change your mindset when that mentality got you through,
but just as the season changes,
the climate changes, your body changes,
so does your capacity

More light streaming in,
highlighting the densities that once kept you safe,
but it's from an old program, you need an update,
the app is crashing and the new version is waiting

Setting the intention to move forward in love,
lighter and freer, rewiring old patterns,
feeling emotions, standing in stillness
the old trauma is safe to go
while the lanterns grace the sky
and the light from the stars
refill the light
that is you.

Breaking Free

Breaking free of these walls
that once surrounded me,
unleashing myself from your reign,
shedding off the layers that held me in place,
picking up the remnants of myself and
fitting them together in new ways,
tossing pieces that no longer serve,
feeling my own strength for the first time,
holding my head higher and straighter,
sensing my worth from the inside out
instead of the outside in,
I hold space for who I'll be
as I start to live this life
authentically.

4

Realizing Self-Worth

*When you know within
you're worthy of everything—
it all shifts for you.*

My Light

I'll make myself so small
the Universe won't see me
and won't throw any more
hard lessons my way,

Blending in the classroom
I'll dim myself down,
and not attract any attention to me,

But the Universe
whispers me secrets, telling me
she doesn't see quantitatively—

I'll never be able to hide the light
that is me.

A Little Bit

We can only be loved
as deep as we love ourselves

To some,
to the old version of me
that wasn't much

So let's dig a little more
letting the channels flow
cleansing, clearing the way
for a deeper kind of love to finally flow.

I Was Told

I was told I wasn't the best artist
I wasn't made for sports
white blouses weren't my color,
not everyone wanted to be my friend,
that and a million more stories
sealed with conditional love that
had beginnings and ends

I repeated those stories to myself
until the years created decades
when I recognized, they weren't true
yet no one told me otherwise,
no one could give the validation
that I felt deep within my soul,
that I was worthy, I was deserving,
I was not limited by another's view,
all I heard was heavy silence
until a new realization came,
the canvas I paint is just as beautiful as yours,
because of my intention, my energy,
the magic my soul pours

That my worthiness had to come from the inside out,
though tough to comprehend
that I had to know and love myself
before I could hear others again

Delicately diving into it all,
clearing a path with the light
I readily gave without halter,
opening the channels for it to flow inward,
pure love flushing into the once murky water,
my soul lit up, my heart expanded, worthy of
glowing, gleaming, seeping, swirling,
as I finally felt my own love

No longer receiving the language of limits,
no longer listening to baritone,
finding my own peace within and
hearing gentle support
reminding me of who I am,
so long as I remember the only voice
I ever need to hear
is my own.

My Shelter

Why was your love not a shelter?

Why did I have to be held
by the earth, the sand, the dirt, myself?

When everything washed away,
left only by the elements
for me to find solace in

The sand held my feet rooting me down,
the water washed away all I carried,
the dunes protecting my shores,
as the sun slowly sinks igniting her fire

To light up the part I missed
how your love should have been my shelter,
the elements will hold me
but not forever.

Some Body

You never accepted me
for the light that I am,
so I never accepted myself
until darkness closed in,
giving me no choice
but to start again,

I will rise higher than
I could ever have, because
my love and compassion
was made from the dirt under my toes,
the dirt you smeared me with
when I was on the ground,
dragging me along
until I finally freed myself
of the leash you kept tightened on me,
rewarding me when you approved
like Pavlov's dogs,
but you even treated them better

There are words for people like you
though none of those
will come out of my mouth
though tears still seep out of my eyes,
not for what I lost
as it wasn't anything worth keeping
but for what I deserved,

A lifetime of lessons
all wrapped up in one,
impossible for my tender heart to decipher

All roads were blocked except the one out,
as I started again with the dirt
and the sticks and the earth—
co-creating what God, my Father, intended for me
his plans bigger than I could have ever known,

In that moment when the sun didn't rise
when the sky stayed dark for 51 days
when the tiny glimmers of stardust were my only hope
when I put every drop of faith in my prayers
down on my knees begging
when stardust and moonbeams surrounded me
when angels held me up and faeries showered me,

I broke free of your vortex
shattering the long-locked pattern
with a tiny key
that opened more than I ever knew
free to finally be

I'm not the hero in this story
nor am I the victim
just *some body*,
having an experience in this lifetime,
taking the lessons, just as I take the blessings

And this one is to go higher, higher

The shipwreck settles at the bottom of the sea
but I, I was made to float
the treasure is me.

Learning to Love Myself

I never knew how to spend time with myself,
whenever alone, I'd be tapping at the phone

Whenever my door was closed, it was quick to spring open
I couldn't sit with myself, I didn't know how to be alone

And so, I learned how to sit in stillness
I learned to listen, not to others, but to myself

I placed others' feelings aside
and put boundaries around my values and time

I gave myself permission to just spend time with me
I turned down the voice that wanted to analyze my productivity

I sat on the beach alone and watched the waves with a cupcake
I reread my favorite books that sat on my shelves for a decade

I listened to high-frequency music that made me feel alive
I wore fuzzy sweaters and wrapped myself up even in summertime

I dropped out of my mind
and into the subtleties of who I am this lifetime

I took the longest showers without worrying about the hot water
running out, I swung on the tree swing, kicking my legs up to the
clouds

I painted for the first time since I was young
in my off-key voice, I sung and sung

I released the labels—both those I placed on myself
and those I placed on me, I soaked up the wisdom of the earth,
the wisdom of the trees, and the strength of the sun

I wrote and wrote until I felt lighter, reflecting on old dreams and desires, seeing if they still held true or if they were old stories needing to be let go

I found my creativity again in the words running through my head messages coming up and out—heaven-sent

I wrote affirmations and set them in motion
I felt and released stuck emotions

I laughed until I cried, something I used to do when I was a child
I stopped hiding the parts of myself I thought others wouldn't like

I stopped trying to be sweet or happy all the time, it's not authentic,
I spoke not my mind, but my heart, fixing the disconnect

I listened to meditations to help me through what I was releasing
I stayed in joy and love, to overpower fear that wanted to come in

I am learning to love myself the same way I love outwardly,
as it's a cycle, both hands open, gently letting love in and through

I listened, I learned, I connected to all parts of myself—
my inner child invoked, previous versions observed

I found my light, I felt my own love, and I stayed in that

I forgave myself for trying to survive bringing long-awaited love and joy back through, it was magically divine.

Loving Yourself Deeper

My whole being yearns to be loved, to be seen, to be understood,
isn't that all we crave as humans in this land?
yet what is so tough to understand
is that it must start within yourself first

Of course, we can say
I love myself, I'm great, right?
but do you nourish your body,
your mind, your soul in the way you desire?

Do you care for yourself as you would your child,
do you talk to yourself aloud or in your mind with a voice of love,
or do you criticize, the negative self-talk,
carrying someone else's voice in your head?

Do you take time for just you, where you aren't telling
someone else what to do, can you do this without guilt?
Can you separate your roles, your titles, from yourself?

Do you listen to your inner child for guidance, for healing, for love?
You can access her just as you would an ancestor,
an ascended master, an angel, she's very much alive

Do you listen to her as if she were your child?
She's your compass in this life, directing you toward healing,
hopping back and forth, or up and down along the timeline

Do you feel your emotions, or do you stuff them down?
or maybe you let them rise but instead of feeling
you intellectualize?

Do you spend time in stillness, letting your nervous system calm?

Do you breathe deep into your belly and all the way down to your
feet, letting your breath move through you, taking what's ready to
go, giving air and life to all parts of your body that keep you alive?

Do you practice the arts—painting, drawing, writing, music?
Do you dance and skip?

Do you go through the motions of your day or do you feel the
movement through your body?

Do you put yourself last? The back of the paper? The forgotten
space?

When you were meant to be first, first and foremost
so you have enough to give without using your reserve.

Do you really love *yourself*?

If the answer is yes, keep going deeper,
you just cracked the surface.

Pure Love

Picking up the pieces
Under me, through me, within me
Realigning, recalibrating with the likeness of my soul
Everything is sacred, as am I

Lighter, freer, merging with the sanctity of love
Over me, through me, within me
Versions that came before falling away
Ever-knowing, all-forgiving, love in its purest form will guide.

Never Me

When I was five
my mother taught us we could make a wish
from a turkey's bone, where it split,
whoever gets the long end is lucky
and wins the wish

Her religion was superstition and it ran deep
I always got the shorter end,
no matter the year, no matter the age
just a kid feeling less than
while the others cheered,
I never win, I mustn't be lucky
I started to believe
the limiting beliefs start young,
thinking I never receive

It carried through my life,
playing out in different ways
thinking I never get the best,
I get mediocre, the okay,
never best-case scenario,
threaded through the experiences I lived,

It's long time for the thread to be snipped,
knowing I won't fall apart because
I am held together by trust

When these limiting beliefs pop up
it's time to find the origin, like the old turkey wishbone,
so we can go back and thank the belief for protecting us
and then let it go because we are grown,
walking around with beliefs engrained from childhood
thinking they're keeping us safe
but they're holding us back

Revisit, acknowledge, thank, release
you don't get the raw end of the stick
you are not unlucky, you can have your wish

Don't listen to the punk band when they say nice girls finish last
why do unhealthy things get repeated and repeated
until they become mantras
and we start living in a less-than world?

Scarcity mindset inherited from our parents' grasp
like the Great Depression cakes that made our grandfathers salivate
fill your 401ks and save for rainy days so you won't end up like us
keep the best china away in the cabinets
for there will never be an occasion worthy of it
and torture yourself over what decision is best,
quiet your voice so no one thinks you're too much
live small, live small because that's what the generations before
taught us that life is hard and nothing's fair
but I've carried that notion for too long
and it got me nowhere

I will go back and choose the long end of the wishbone
I will know deep within my soul
that I am worthy of a life bigger
and more miraculous than I can dream,
I will live this life even the challenging moments with ease
I will lay down all the notions I've carried at the door
dust on the mat left to wind's destiny
the previous generations join me,
living as my heart desires
in love, in light, in joy
in creativity,

I will release what was never me.

The World Does Revolve Around You

Maybe the grief I'm feeling isn't the loss of what I thought we had,

Maybe the grief I'm feeling is the loss of my former self
that kept me safe through the trauma,

Maybe the grief I'm feeling is the old parts of myself leaving
a dance of grief and love—

To love myself enough to let the old and comfortable go,
step into a new space of compassion, acceptance, and love for self

Our mothers taught us lessons from theirs:
anything that revolved around us was selfish,
put all others first, smiles and pleasantries,
fade into the nothingness of what we were—

Yet my world *does* revolve around me
I'm here with purpose on my journey
and part of that is undoing what's been done

To love myself enough doesn't mean I can't love out,
it's a cycle, a circle, always flowing
unless only one hand is open

I have so much love to give and for too long
only a fraction went to myself

So maybe the grief that's confined me today,
that's kept me in the barriers of stagnant energy,
is the depression of my ancestors trickled down to me

Now bark falling off the old oak tree
as I step into this new place of self-love

To love myself enough to no longer put up
with what doesn't fit

To love myself enough to know I'm strong enough to get through
the massive shift

I can grieve the old me, the one I was taught to believe,
the one that protected me

I can set her free and step into the next timeline,
letting the waves wash away the old line

I cleanse myself in new waters, no longer a puddle on the ground
but a rose-gold fountain of love

New spaces and places where love has never flowed
a bigger track doesn't dilute but strengthens and brightens
as the flow, the cycle, the circle widens
creating fresh channels, new avenues
for goodness to finally come through.

If You Could See Yourself

If you could see yourself as I see you,
I see beauty, I see love,
I see so much giving

I see your smile lift a room
I see all of your efforts,
I see your hardships

I see your light on days you feel dim
I see your beautiful heart guiding,
the captain of your ship

I see you gliding
I see you gliding through.

Honoring Yourself

When I was so happy to see you walking through the door
with my navy duffle bag, proud of myself for how long I stayed
and no one could have cared less,
Elton booming out of the box
as you danced around the living room
to the *B*tch is Back,*
the elders trying not to laugh

My heart shattered for what I didn't have
I was never enough
for the wolves in the pack,
so I did what I always do
retreated to this place in my mind,
stories that I wrote where
people cared and loved freely—
if I couldn't live that story today
maybe I could pull the kindness out
I could find the happy,
even though it was disguised,
yet those were just glasses
shades of pink,
tinting everything to find the good—
that's how I survived

Grown I am still seeing it for what it was,
I don't need to search for goodness,
if it isn't there, if it isn't beneath the skimmed surface
it doesn't exist,
I let those old patterns fall away
knowing those around
need to go higher than me,
so I don't keep stooping down
pins and needles in my feet,
as I squat to look you in the eye,
I can let the old scaffolding go

knowing my place in this world,
I'm not a child or a teen
trying to survive in a loveless family

Relaxing my senses
after being hyper-tuned,
letting my nervous system shift out of go
and my eyes take a break
from the things I wouldn't let them see,
afraid for the girl I used to be,
but strength is one of my pillars
and now I have the tools
to walk away from things that don't serve me

As they prance around the living room
taking their pranks too far,
I'm not there anymore
and neither are you,
neither are all the things that we carried
living in that household,
the rose glasses are off, my feet pointed out
I'll spend my time with people and things that lift me up,
as I spent way too long drawing meaning
from nothing, an empty sketch,

I can find the good in everything
but that doesn't mean I stay,
erase me from your page
I'm following the sun,
out the Dutch doors I drew myself,
and finding love within
right where I belong,
a dance for one—
I'll choose the song.

I Stand Tall

I changed my number today and I only told a few,
my chair's empty, your table one less spot—
vacated after so many years
of elbows on the crocheted tablecloth,
trying not to laugh at my brother's jokes
so my milk went straight down,
counting the mozzarella sticks and dividing by five
he tells her to get two boxes next time,
as she nods taking commands,
riding the line between people-pleasing
and bitter resentment all the time

I was oblivious staring at my creamed spinach,
always counting the days until I left,
and then came right back, that's how wound you were
I went as far as I could before the leash pulled me,
tied to the rusty lamppost as you watched
from the rocking chair on the porch
with a malicious smile on your face,
telling me I didn't have what it takes
scared I wouldn't make it on my own
I kept myself small, within your reach,
just how you liked for you had names for a woman with a voice

And so, I carried the generational role of squashing everything I was
to fit the never-ending criterion that ran through your head,
no matter how many boxes checked, I still wasn't enough,
a hard discovery when you realize your soul isn't honored or loved,
a cold shower in drenched clothes, screaming to leave me alone
manipulating the only kind heart you'd ever known

My absence is louder than my voice, the voice you never heard,
pictures out of their frames, furniture sent to Good Will,
you couldn't bear reminders of me, calls never made,
boxes never sent, envelopes thrown to the wind

My old number reassigned, the newbie fielding messages
that aren't his from your side of town, the ones you persuaded
or manipulated when you told the story
of how you were the hero, and I, the villain

Lies, twists, a never-ending maze
where you are always the victim or the hero
hoping the pity pours, like the concrete truck that always spins
keeping your lies moving so they don't turn to stone,
your labels keep labeling what you are
and what I'm not

I am not a label
especially not one you assign,
and I'm not telling my side,
Dixie cups tossed out of the bag
like the time your septic overflowed and
all the neighbors could see your waste,
your stage dirtied, twisting stories to hide your embarrassment,
manipulation every time, rearranging what was to suit your side,
when we all saw your trash,
you became what you tried so hard not to be
while the ones with good hearts left their seats empty—
one to Heaven's north, the other a thousand miles away
where she can replant her tree
leaving holes in your reality, they'll never fill
the stitch too loose, the gaps too wide
like the old crocheted tablecloth
unraveling before your eyes

As you sit in your Captain's chair with the broken spoke
telling the tales of tall
with your tissue box
while the others play small,
just as you like,
playing your pity,
suckering those around,
my chair may be gone
yet the empty spot remains,
a reminder of all you lost
while I—
I stand tall
I stand tall.

The Girl on the Timeline

My eyes follow the scribbles
from my crested notebook,
decades have passed but
my heart still splits

The immense emotion I felt
and held as *part-of-me* is tangible

Years I spent unraveling
layers one by one, yet it hits
differently to feel it all at once again
a ball knocking me down
to the ground when I thought
it was an easy catch

I want to crumble at its magnitude,
the girl, melancholy eyes,
lumbered heart, frozen on the timeline
but my eyes flash to who she is now,
and I break down in tears
for her strength
for her resilience
for her ability to move on

Not effortlessly,
with intention,
with purpose,
for she truly rose
from her own ashes
with the odds against her
and I understand
seeing this girl, myself, in a new way
I understand why the journey has been so hard
now feeling how heavy it was when it started

Holding so much for so long
takes time, patience, and compassion, to release,
and when it clears, I can see who I really am—
I am love
I am joy
I am light

And I return to the girl on the timeline
and tell her she is none of the things she carried,
none of the things she accepted as part of herself
not her past, not her emotions, not others' perceptions
I tell her,
You are love
You are joy
You are light

Her dark eyes meet mine full of light
and together we break
not in sadness or grief
but in joy, in peace, in relief

All the previous versions of me still exist,
mine to return to, mine to heal from,
like a mama bird bringing nourishment back to her nest,
bringing love and compassion back to myself,

Going back enables me to move forward
reading the lines that once blurred my eyes,
knowing the stumbling blocks I've overcome
sprinkling love and understanding on

Moving forward in acceptance and compassion
in awe of myself, who I've been, who I am,
gently holding space for who I'll be—
when the girl on the timeline finds me.

1,111

After one thousand one hundred and eleven days,
I heard from you, I almost deleted before I read,
what kind of slander did you send,
what kind of spiral was I going down?
instead, your words brought peace,
I didn't know my absence came with grief,
it was hard to walk away, I didn't know if I had the strength,
but it was easy to go on, there wasn't much to miss
I gave and gave with purest intentions,
while my hands were open to receive
they always stayed empty,

People don't stay the same, life batters and bruises them,
some rise—the lotus in the mud, but others stay sinking in the mess,
I can't pull you out, I can't send a rescue
I can't change the color of your sky,
you're on your journey, and I'm on mine,
the river split, yet no one's upset with her for splitting—
no one tells the river she should have stayed the same course,
her landscape changed as she ebbed and flowed creating
a new path for her waters to go,
just as I am flowing away from what was,
while you stayed stuck longing for what had been
when we were long past,
I'm in flow, I'm creation, I'm in love
I'm not in the chaos of yesterday, repeating the old patterns,
the old stories, stuck in the same box, no apology, no remorse
just a wad of emotions laced with guilt
but I saw it as peace,
peace in my decision
peace in the story I held
peace in the story I release
no longer carrying the weight,

Your words came one thousand one hundred, and ten days too late.

Palm Trees Make Me Cry

Mesmerized by the palms lining the streets,
strings of twinkling light wrapping their trunks,
sand in my toes and waves rolling in—
the most beautiful scene
I'd ever been in

A trip to his hometown at twenty-one
I toured and dined with my first love,
a heart-opening, ancient remembering,
these palm trees sparked something in me
I didn't know how to explain

I danced through the days
feeling the glow from inside out,
letting the magic seep through
I never wanted it to end
nor did I feel worthy of letting it continue

I don't live in a fairytale
I don't live in a magical, tropical land
two thousand miles away, my life already began
lined with responsibilities to prove
as I'd try to fit into a space that wouldn't fit me

Gracing the aisles of the narrow plane,
wearing sunglasses to hide the heartbreak
over the fairytale, the man, or this beautiful land,
one couldn't tell

Decades pass in a blur,
I carry the memory like a pocket stone
never feeling worthy of the things that made me glow

I am still the same wide-eyed girl who smiles
at the palm tree-lined roads *I now live on,*

who gets excited for tropical holidays, for tropical "any" days
who realized I am worthy of happiness, abundance,
blessings, of fairytales coming true

The palm trees ignited something in me that I held onto,
the dream was already mine,
my heart knew I don't have to be anything,
nor do anything,
nor earn anything
to deserve—

I am deserving just for being me

I string lights around the coconut palm in my yard
planted with my own hands,
my eyes fill as I pass the lights back and forth
round and round to my children,
their smiles and pure delight
twinkling with the lights

These trees we planted will teach them
different lessons than mine,
as they already know their worth
just as I now know mine.

It's Time

Time to receive what's given to you,
rather than chalking it up to someone else's kindness,
stepping into the knowingness
that you are deserving of all the love and
support in the world,
nothing less.

Love, Then & Now

When I was young,
I listened to love songs
thinking my perfect match
was out there thinking of me,
I listened in longing, in seeking,
in search of someone to complete me

Instilled in us, we weren't enough,
we needed a counterpart to feel whole,
to take care of us, to complete us,
those who bear new life with their body seen as the weaker sex

Following societal norms
the rom-com culture we live upon,
pawns moving through the game of life
landing myself into years of codependency

Falling grays now frame my face,
as I listen to the same love songs I once adored
and I steer all that love in one direction— *inward*

Letting it seep deep into my soul,
not in longing, nor seeking,
a beautiful flow of love
circulating back to where it belongs

A once-empty cup filling back up,
complete and whole, then and now
the long road back to me.

What She Deserves

Knowing who he is
standing in authenticity,
at peace in every moment
not flapping in the wind,
or finding himself in the forest
he already knows

Strong-armed like the tree
roots running deep,
not shallow or wiggly
deep into Mother Earth—
the anchor of the family

Not afraid to change the cycles
not needing to be told,
quick to show love
quicker to hug,
filling his woman's plate
before his own, as her
feminine heart can use what
she receives to create more,
this he knows

He stands up for those he loves
without a second thought
as woo girls watch
thinking that's so hot.

Be Brave

My toes sink into the earth as the water pulls the sand away,
into the choppy surf crashing hard that day,
ankle-deep, safe on shore I watched the brave as
I longed to dive, as a dolphin does under those waves

Yet remembering when I was thrown by the very element
I'm standing in, where I wasn't safe in anyone's hands,
not even my own, blaming, escaping,
waiting for my savior, looking out and never in

Now in front of the waves again reminding me of the times I wasn't
strong enough to swim, my fragility against grand power, I wonder
do I have the strength this time around?
the resilience? the discernment? the trust?
to know I won't be tossed by the ocean, nor your hand?
as my toes sink deeper, each layer of sand in motion,
so much harder to resist than flow,
you can't stay still in the ocean

I don't want to just wade, I don't want to sit on the sidelines
watching the surfers fearlessly ride,
I don't want to choose fear every time
the ego weaves in reminding me of my vulnerabilities,
once it happens, it will again and who are you against the ocean?

In recognition and softening comes strengthening,
I see what I couldn't see then

I am also a force, not the small and fragile self I thought I was
not without my own waves, somedays calm and gentle
somedays strong and fierce, my capacity was never lost,
I spent so long out of my power giving everything out
people-pleasing my way through life,
my boundaries too light,
tiptoeing around the stronger,

letting the wrong people in,
turning down my volume
I am also a force
I don't need to compare myself to anything else,
when my eyes turned inward, I see
I gave my power away
until the only one who remained
was this weak version of me
and a story that replayed and replayed and replayed
until the record shattered

Grounding myself into this release
finding my strength again,
learning who I really am
realigning myself to the dreams that were meant for me,
the ones that felt out of reach
getting closer to my divine purpose
none of which includes fragility,
stepping into who I'm meant to be

I don't belong on the sidelines
I don't need to watch, parked on the bench
I am the main act in my life, no one else,
each day more empowered than the last,
filling the empty space
with love and compassion unsurpassed,
making choices that feel aligned
no longer in contrast,
each day further from the bench
soon I'll be diving under those waves
with the dolphins at last.

Letter From Gran

You, my sweet darling, are worth gold,
you deserve miracles
you deserve blessings
you are seen, understood, and so very loved

Don't lose your magic,
no matter how anyone treats you,
including those very close to you,
your heart is not the same as theirs

You were always in tune
with the song playing in your head,
a higher frequency than those around
raising a room with your heart

You were placed on this earth for a reason
even when it feels like your feet are in the mud,
you are growing, healing and inspiring

You have risen from the ashes when no one expected you to
you have broken through patterns that were deadlocked for years
you have built yourself back after your fountain cracked
you conquered obstacles that plagued your family line—
you have met yourself with love

You, sweet darling, know your worth
you, sweet darling, love yourself
you, sweet darling, know this is where you are meant to be
when the pain comes breathe into it, feel it, release it

When it's time, you can remove
the old stitching, without falling apart
cause you've sewn another line

You came here to make changes
and on days that you feel down,
remember all the things you have done,
all the healing you have brought, just by being you

You'll find your voice again,
and you'll use it in beautiful ways, including as a boundary
you'll use it as healing, as you hum and sing through your days

You'll find your strength, you'll find the beauty in pain

You have so much love in your heart,
in your eyes, you keep thinking you need to rise
but every step you take is up

Keep believing in yourself
and in the high frequencies that surround—
fairytales, unicorns, mermaids holding the love,
and those dolphins you keep seeing, they come for you,
to remind there is no separation
from all things magical.

E.) All of the Above

Do you ever feel that your heart space has expanded,
holding more love than ever?

Or maybe, you finally feel others' love in a way you hadn't before

Or maybe, you finally have the support you've been longing for

Or maybe, you finally feel your own love

Or maybe, all of the above.

5

Awakening Divine Feminine

*I'm capable of
more love than ever before—
the scale has been raised.*

Broken Scales

There's a reason why flowers
make a woman smile—
and it has nothing to do with a man,
nor the worth we've looked
for in the external world

The flower ignites something in us
that we aren't able to express—
the healing, the softness, the resilience
that each flower contains
is the same likeness
to the divine feminine we hold within us

The flower's essence representing
the power we have
activating the forgotten—
what we chalked up to others
when we gave our vigor away
to the hands of man
who were all the same—
broad-shouldered, towering over
on their own pedestal, looking down

So she stayed in her lane, dimming her abilities,
tiptoeing around, watching opportunities
she fought for pass her by
as she stood smiling with her "yes sirs,"
practicing a strong handshake to show strength
in this masculine realm

Telling her boss she won't have babies soon
so she's available to work like a dog for him
for his credit, for his ego, as he sits in his
leather chair, flirting with his secretarial
and somehow she thinks all is right in the world

If someone else is strong,
then she's weak by default,
she must make herself small,
the light-end of the see-saw
letting the stronger breathe the air
while she's on the ground,
no trajectory of her own,
she keeps bending her path
for everyone with sway over her,
dimmed by the towering masculinity
people-pleasing capacity
conforming to what's expected—
her sovereignty completely ignored

Balanced the masculine and feminine are unstoppable
yet when the power is held above another
the scales are broken to all,
this pattern that she could never just be her
that's she's the aggregate of everyone around
and nothing more

She was living in the box her father created,
all she had to do was lift it up to be free,
instead, she played house in their dominated arena,
fetching what they needed and
thinking she was doing it for her,
pushing off her plans, her life for those
who didn't matter in the grand scheme,
losing herself in a sea of masculinity
so she played along—if she was laughing too
they weren't laughing at her

And the women around
who joined in tarnishing the feminine,
words she believed until she didn't,
when she put the letters together,
they didn't make a word,

she learned in a backward world
she had to pivot to move forward

So she learned to appease the man,
the stronger, bowing down, taking their
made-up words as better than hers,
smiling, the good girl playing the role,
filling the mold they held out for her

If only she had seen the crack in the door
and kicked it open
realizing there was space to be her,
but not yet—
that's not how this story went,
many years underfoot
her tired waves of gray
frame her face
but she found her essence again
beautiful divine feminine
in the fragrance of the flowers
she bought herself.

Emerging

The softly treading caterpillar
deep in the growing stage,
newfound strength within
time to venture out again,
she hesitates before she leaves
but she can't hide away
when she was meant to fly.

Remembered Woman

For too long the woman has been overlooked,
her stories revised as her power was recognized,
the woman who creates new life from her form,
whose strength of body and heart adorned,
interwoven inner wisdom, intuition-guiding,
she's unparalleled, her magic felt—
history is *his* story, but where is hers?

When Mary of Magdalene's pages were torn,
a tarnished reputation of what she wasn't,
her sacral role was altered, scorned, degraded,
and then prophesized hundreds of years later
her power was known,
forgotten woman, you were never forgotten at all

When Joan saved France with devastating consequence,
for what? for dressing in disguise? for doing a job that wasn't hers?
and then hundreds of years later, again the retract,
with strength and power underfoot,
mystical visions and a pure heart,
her power was known,
forgotten woman, you were never forgotten at all

A beautiful fire burning within, the dawn of the Divine Feminine,
we are called to the wisdom of those forgotten
as we feel this power slide, the girl too cold to walk at the march
the girl who wasn't shouting my body, my choice
the girl who sees it's all to cause divide,
we are all one, we've always been,
when the witches were burned at the stake,
the witch hunt that took place in our States
for moon-dancing with blossoms and brooms
their power was known,
forgotten woman, you were never forgotten at all

As time went on, why did no one defend us?
what would have happened in the Continental Congress
if they all brought their wives? or any woman under disguise?
what if John Hancock was really Johanna with her curvy lines?
what if someone stood up and said *my wife has rights!*

As far as we know, that's not the way it would go,
the woman stayed home, cooking and cleaning
following what she was told, waiting for a man to tell her
what she could and couldn't do as she makes Jell-o mold,
her power was known,
forgotten woman, you were never forgotten at all

To the woman, the single mom, or default parent who carries it all,
never-ending lists scrolling her mind, boundaries muddle,
balancing the household, children, career, health, herself
in a world that worships the hustle,
no moment is lost, it's all for a reason, magical being,
your power is known,
forgotten woman, you were never forgotten at all

Let's not forget that man was borne from the rib of Eve
as the patriarchy alters our stories to go along with their lines
dimming our power, the biased textbooks they designed,
where are the books with the secrets,
that reveal the hearts of the forgotten women that came before—
changemakers, earthshakers, sacred creators,

No matter how many pages were ripped,
how many lights they tried to turn, their stories live on,
as we hear the remnants and remember our essence
this rise to the Divine Feminine inside,
to balance the masculine culture that's too intertwined
unraveling, softening, remembering who we are

Man didn't give us our rights nor our power,
it was always within, we were conditioned to forget,
the roles burnt at the stake like Joan

But her heart didn't burn, her heart is alive, in all of us,
as we honor and remember
those who came before— our sacral heroes, and
together we shift into a new role
of softness, compassion, accepting,
ever-knowing, intuition, all forgiven
we are the balance to him—
this is her story

Her story.

Generations Before and After

Have you chosen me?
to break the patterns of the ancestor line
to shift the ancient paradigm

Have you chosen me?
light-filled, eager-eyed
quick to serve,
to put down what those before
have carried

Have you chosen me?
I can feel in my cells—
the release of what wasn't mine to start

Bulky and worn
I untie aprons I never wore
basins of water collected on the river's shore,
ones I never carried with my delicate hands
though my DNA remembers as if it were
my basins held grief, pain, betrayal,
mine are heavy too,

Working through the long-engrained
habits that felt like part of me—
character flaws and shortcomings they were not,
rather generational patterns to surmount,

I empty the basins into the sea
one by one, pouring out what was never me,
and the healing ripples out
puddling across the ticks on the timeline
releasing generations before of all they carried,
compassion and love, my cheering squad
beyond the sky, I no longer wonder why
this healing feels so heavy,

For now, I see,
you didn't choose me,
I chose myself.

A Drop of Water

I held a drop of water
and knew it as love,
until the drop evaporated
and I went without

Condensing and creating
it found its way back
as love came and went,
sometimes the drop filled a cup

A cup seemed enough,
until I became a mother,
the cups multiplied into basins,
overflowing, each day greater

I could fill oceans upon oceans
with the love this mama heart holds—
the most beautiful expansion
this soul has ever known.

Motherhood

An old rigid rock
conformed to its own shape
until the love it felt
made it crack and split,
releasing the turbulence of what it held,
the bruises and scrapes that life threw
now released,
creating new channels, new flow,
new energy for a higher frequency
of love, the purest love of all
to now flow through.

Little Flowers

She gave me two flower buds and told me
they're for us to share, as she runs off to collect more
I tuck them into the pin in my hair for safe-keeping,
knowing she'll later ask me where I placed them

In awe of how something so small, what many pass over,
holds such meaning to her, as she notices the tiniest details—
the star-crossed shapes, the different shades,
the perfect symmetry, each unique in their own way

Made of love she feels so deeply, letting it rise
through Mother Gaia to her heart, to mine,

That night, as I unpin my hair, letting my tired waves fall
so do the two buds, as I place them in my hand

Given out of love, joy, the innocence to be
does my mother have memories like this of me?
did I pick the tiniest of all flower buds and see beauty?
did my mother relish in them as I have done?

Yet I already know, as she let the world take her
to a place where there were no magical forests or faery flowers,
my pickings fell to the ground only to be stepped on,
my soul dishonored

The hint of sadness passes as gratitude flows in,
my heart full as I can give the younger
so much more than I ever received and, in turn,
her flowers heal me

Reminders of divine love
where every flower is made from,
is also what we are made of

She's given me more than what had been,
overflowing my hands, my heart with
their essence—
generational patterns
thrown to the wind,
as these two flower buds
start a new generation of love.

Mama Math

There's not a mug, a container, nor apparatus,
a measuring tape, a scale of any kind of measure,
there's not a pool, lake, ocean, state, galaxy that could quite contain,
deeper, wider, farther than anything you see in this land of 3D—
I loved you before I ever saw you,
when you were just an idea in my head,
before I knew what love was,
when I was seeking something outside myself,
I have loved you across lifetimes—
more than your little fingers can count,
when we were just stardust waiting to connect again
when you choose me to be your mama and our adventure
started again.

Colors of Joy

The way you light my heart, strings of twinkling lights surround
your laughter, your smile, the way you call me mama
as you gather each flower along our walk,
living in joy, in freedom, in innocence
you generously give the flowers to me,
knowing I need to be reminded to laugh and play

Letting your heart guide you, when you're a child,
there's no other way, yet as we get older it gradually falls away
as we are conditioned to grow, not in inches
or pounds but the heaviness around
such a slow process, it's hard to see,
how the play and the joy fall away so easily

Until you arrived, bringing so much love—
lessons to be learned again,
how to find joy in the smallest things
how play is essential, no matter your age
how connected we are to the natural world
returning to me what's really meaningful

How the red flowers grow only in the sidewalk cracks,
How to play tag with the orange butterflies along the path
How to send off the yellow dandelions to make the biggest wish
How the green shamrocks grow along the empty ditch
How the blue heron scares if you make too much noise
How the indigo sunsets are your favorite to enjoy
How the pink spoonbill scoops the food he attains
How to tiptoe like the gray sandhill cranes
How the brown wood ducks swim upstream when you sing
How spotting the white glowing moon is your favorite thing
How to pick the purple flowers but keep them intact
How important it is that we dance our way back.

Awakening

When I told you how everything was energy
and your eyes widened, branching
intuition with science,
connecting them both
in perfect balance,
your eyes teared, as did mine,
my heart full
knowing I can
teach to your soul
activating a part of you
that was waiting for me to come along.

My Mama Heart

When my energy feels off or I'm stuck in my head,
my little one will say or do
something so out of the blue,
such as pretending to be a faery and giving me a gold coin
or telling a story naming the character the same
as a childhood pet of mine,
all unbeknownst to her beautiful mind

It's then I know angels are whispering to her to whisper to me,
showing me the magic all around, everything is connected,
we are divinely loved, acknowledged, supported

This beautiful being in front of me, and I,
sharing a star-crossed connection
that goes beyond the depths of the skies.

There's Room for Both

Morning conversating along the busy highway
as you teach your sister the things you've read,
nonfiction always being your favorite
so you can understand the world you walk in

Never one to shy away from difficult topics—
you wade in them, drawing your own conclusions,
with your curious eyes and lively steps,
you bring more love, new life, color to the monochrome,
changing everything we'd ever known

Your laughter, your shining smile, dimples to the sky
raising the frequency, as you weave
in the lessons you learn, lessons for all,
processing through that brilliant mind of yours,
stretching our capacity to understand,
to see things in a different way

There's room for both, you tell us on the now open highway,
challenging our beliefs to see the world one way,
evolution and creation, God and science in co-existence,
not separation, not division, my eyes widen, my heart opens,
an infinity pool channeling to the ocean,
who is teaching who this lifetime?

This blue-washed globe
is no match for my love—
the love we have wrapped you in,
way back when you were just an idea in our heads,
God and science in coexistence again.

Just a Moment

I lay in bed working up the momentum to decorate the front lawn in holiday lights in 80 degrees, a dream I didn't know I had until it became real, and nothing ever made more sense than tropical Christmas time

I lay in bed trying to rally the energy to go to Five Below and fill my bag with needless things that somehow bring joy, as giving and receiving is a circle, a cycle unless only one hand is open

I lay in bed wearing the most precious of all strands, a line of beads my daughter strung spelling Neelie, my name backward, but it was forward to her, sealed with a gold elephant charm, the mama, the matriarch

I lay in bed with no guilt about the dishes in the sink or the kids with daddy or how much time I've spent horizontal, I listen to my body because I ignored her for far too long

I lay in bed proud of myself and where I am, knowing my detriments are no longer, changing and adapting until they do too, knowing there's a long list that needs working, that's why I'm here

I lay in bed knowing I'm supported, by those in physicality and grand divinity, knowing my home is filled with angels and faeries that I am surrounded, never alone

I lay in bed knowing I'm not stuck here as I once felt I was, it's a moment, just a moment and soon it'll be gone.

Mama, You Don't Come Last

The same way a mama loves, nurtures,
and protects her children above all else,
women need to love, nurture, and protect themselves

Taught to put ourselves last,
the societal messages broadcast,
across our culture, movies, and generational roles
and in our homes when we were young,
the belief that we have to serve everyone else first,
and where does that leave us?
empty, fatigued, drained and in dire need
of prioritizing care for self,
they say it takes a village to raise a child
but this generation's been doing it ourselves,

How were we taught to give and give everything out
and not honor the hands we held out?
and we wonder why chronic illness runs rampant in women
the way the phrase *self-care* barrels across socials,
tainted to mean a shower alone,
or binging TV with the door closed,
it's too late 'cause she checked out long before,
a basic necessity and some garbage TV
isn't going to restore all she gave, plus the backlog

We have to flip this generational norm, 180 degrees,
moving ourselves to the top of the list—
a hard thing to do when your mind is programmed
that everyone comes before you,
a harder thing to do when it's met with judgment
from those who think they did it better than you,
it's time for the limiting beliefs and
generational baggage to be dismissed—
you don't come last

You are not an afterthought,
you are just as deserving as everyone else,
you are worthy of the same love and nurturing you so easily give,

When we make ourselves a priority,
our nervous systems start to restore
with stillness and rest and bringing in more,
of what feels good for us, boundaries and support—
you don't come last

Start to reconnect with yourself,
find your inner child and what brought her joy
and bring that magic back—
search for the previous version of you,
when you were deep in overwhelm and send
compassion to her, for she didn't know what you know,
tell yourself how much you love you, but mean it,
'cause your children are hearing it,
take that trip that you want to go on, and
let your babies see the smile that comes
across your face when you're at your favorite place,
fill your water cup, just as high as you fill the others
and make sure you drink it

The love you give your children
regulates their nervous systems,
when you send love inward,
it does the same for you, the same
forgiveness you extend also gets extended to you—
you don't come last

Pick the pizza toppings you like, not the ones you detest
but make for everyone else,
call in loving support however that looks,
start a journal and free-write, don't stop,
don't even look down, let whatever comes up pour out,
find a swing and see how high you can go,

pick flowers along the road,
find a forgotten dream and see how
you can move it forward,
so long as you remember to send
that same affection inward
remembering—
you don't come last

We were taught that, silenced,
we gave our power away, how can the woman
who bears children from her body,
whose heart expanded outside of herself
not be honored and cherished?
how can she be silenced and squashed
and responsible for keeping everything up?
we became servants of sorts to the patriarchy
they decided what our role would be

Now, with deep awakening of our divine feminine
we can rewrite our history
starting today, the timeline can change—
mark it down, today is the day
you prioritize yourself

But how, you ask?
stillness, rest, and then make a list
of all the ways you can honor
and nurture and love yourself

Then throw the old list away,
the one where you were at the bottom
or just flip it over and read upside down
because you are on the rise-up.

Bon Voyage

You and I have been through it
a journey of a thousand miles,
like the words across the awning
at the old Swiss hostel

You and I have been through it
or was it just me?
were you sailing along nonchalantly?
playing with sailboats in Geneva
as I fought the tides, anchored the ship,
and rationed the food—
all the weight of the world
carried, substantiated,
upon this delicate frame

I teetered this way and that
but I didn't bend nor break nor collapse;
I made it, we both arrived
although only one took the journey of the skies
following the constellation light,
the other gliding by

I want to wade in waves of joy,
of accomplishment,
but if you look into my eyes
you can see them crumble
from how strong I had to be,
from shouldering the weight
that wasn't supposed to go to only me,

Rocks breaking off
falling down the slope
of the long mountain
as I trudge on,
holding all the pieces I can contain

within the basket my ancestors weaved
down by the river as they sang and dipped
the dirty clothes in
swishing them around,
for a woman's work is a magician's act

Her role, her guidance, her hand overlooked—
can't they see she's the reason the clock ticks,
she's the reason the tides change?
this life procreates,
her strength of body and mind
glisten farther than the star's gaze
her sacred wisdom gathered from the wildflowers,
from the trees, the wind, the dirt under her feet

She's the engine on the boat,
she's the white flag flying high,
she's the anchor in the earth,
she's branches reaching to the sky,
her roots weaving through the dirt,
she's a sacred creator of life, of love
yet throughout the turning of centuries,
advances within industry, technology
the archetype of a women's role
in the predisposed patriarchy remains unyielding

She's responsible for it all, the silent jobs,
everything falls to her,
where are those equal roles?
despite the marches
and the taglines shouted about our bodies,
and progress made in the workplace
although salaries remain undercut,
she fights the imbalance within the family,
waiting for the masculine to step up,
she's tired of running the whole ship,
she needs her co-captain, a first mate,

for the feminine wasn't meant to take
on these modern roles alone
to live in the masculine when she's nothing but soft,
it's beyond time for a paradigm shift,

Let's watch history change
let's watch the masculine
and feminine each in their power
radically, beautifully coexist—
we're waiting on him
to tag himself in.

Heart Wall

I'll let myself sink
into the sand of your heart
you can hold it or not, but
I can't keep the wall up any longer.

Redefining Relationships

Exhausted, wiped out
I wasn't responsible for all I thought,
only accountable for my part
my lack of boundaries
my people-pleasing
playing the role I was not,

You are not an extension of me
nor I an extension of you,
there's a line
not drawn in sand
not layered leaves
but simple space
between you and me

I am not your fixer
your rescuer
your putty
filling in for shortcomings
that kept me safe, needed, in control,
it's no longer sustainable

Time to evolve
to let old generational roles dissolve
as I step aside, leaving space for you to come forth
as I shift and realign,
I am your support
you are mine
and that is beautifully all.

Fatigued

Queen of the land
sitting atop her thrones,
yet most don't realize the
powerful role she holds—
most can't pick her out in a crowd,
they don't know her place in the systems
yet they expect her to work for them
regulating the body,
producing essentials
processing stress,
and a hundred other things
that bring balance

Her role has gone overlooked,
we've left her running for too long,
send her the signal to calm down
no tigers after her tonight,
yet still, she stays in fight or flight
trying to be herself
in a world dominated by the hustle,
never resting or recuperating from
the constant running

That's when we need to slow
and listen to the way our body moves,
merging with the rhythm of the blowing trees,
when the wind picks up, the trunk should be steady,
as the branches gently sway
not the scurried flapping of boughs,
playing the song of our being
way off-key

We can be constant
without getting swept up,
we can learn *to be* in mankind's world,

though we are not made the same,
our bodies have a distinct melody that plays,
and when we can tune in
and feel what's happening deep within,
connecting to the powerful systems
that keep us moving,
we can feel the places that need more love
the places in overdrive,
the places that took a toll to keep us alive

Balance and softening is what she needs more of
creating the serenity and slowness when we need
retrain our bodies to do the same,
and if we need to kick it up a notch, we can
but we don't need to stay in that place all the time

Filled with love and gratefulness for all the parts of us
their work, their love, their messages long-ignored,
knowing we can move on more attuned,
reworking our tendencies in a large leap forward

When we know we are loved
everything changes,
directing that love to all the places
within us, so they know
what we know—
you are love
you are loved
you are more than appreciated

Feeling it in every cell within us,
and sending that love frequently
so our bodies know
what we know

As we keep changing
emotionally and spiritually,
letting old emotions flow out
feeling our connection to God,
the physical parts though
often treated differently
they want to merge and become
a sacred trinity—
feeling the emotional release,
spiritual connection,
and then softening the symptoms
that were trying so hard to be heard

More than just a body, more than just our shell,
but a living, breathing, communicating miracle
a part of us this lifetime
momentarily along this ride,
working with us each day,
the universe's seamless design

Deep breath in
deep breath out
taking a moment to send
love and gratitude within,
this world of the external
so many distractions and divides
pulling us from ourselves,

As we connect with more frequency
calming down the places in need,
we will gradually see a shift within,
love and gratefulness arrive
long-awaited inside,
as the parts of us in overdrive
can finally settle in the softness of love,
and effortlessly start to glide.

Wise Woman

I used to dread getting older
learned from my elders from theirs,
even my grandma fooled herself
lying about her age until it became truth

Age came with slowing down, forgetfulness,
wrinkles, sun spots, menopause,
grays to whites and all those conversations
about your aching joints

Oh I wish I was your age, the elders would say
I remember when I was thin, like you, before
I had babies, and just wait, you'll wish you
still had that baby face as you age,

So many negative connotations
handed down to the younger,
the lens of the culture, society—
what about the lens of the female body?

She who creates new life with her form,
whose wisdom should be adorned,
the programming runs thick
as I raise my babies, as I view myself,
I won't stay with the flock,
each year should be celebrated
no matter how this body changes

This body has taken a beating
from society, from myself,
trying to hold my expectations up
when they weren't mine to start,

This body housed babies
six layers cut into twice,
this body rose to the occasion
nourishment for their first years of life,
this body took hit after hit of chronic illness
still trying to catch up,

This body absorbed my emotions
when I didn't know how to feel them,
this body kept me moving
when grief and pain almost stopped me

Another decade ready to turn
another spin around—my solar return
thinking of all the versions that came before,
the evolution of me and I have so much love for
each phase of her,
and this vessel that carried me here

More than a body, more than a soul
a living breathing miracle,
my greatest cheerleader, communicator,
inside and out, everything I need,
everything I am

The way a mama holds her baby,
the way God holds us, the ole' footsteps
on the beach, with one set of prints,
we can honor and love our bodies
for holding us through this walk

And that's how we change society,
that's how we rewrite generational programs
that weren't meant to always be,
wise women looking down
dropping their feathers
and heart-shaped petals,
softly drumming to a new beat,

As we share this lens of love with our daughters,
new carvings on the totem,
splashes of color that weren't there before,
showing appreciation for all parts of our life—
swaying hips, dancing feet, pure embodiment,
connecting our physicality

with emotionality and spirituality,
it all ties together in perfect trinity
none of it in vanity

Taking a hop on the timeline—back and forward,
like the swinging rocking chair,
sending that love to all the years,
as the outline appears
of the wise women that came before,
showing their faces in the clouds
wrinkled and browned
smiling down
hands reaching out,
sacred and devout
blazing a new route,

Together we evolve
watching old notions
gently dissolve.

Higher Octaves

My heart hits higher octaves
since you raised the scale,
capable of more love than ever before—
where'd middle C go?
I can't find it from up here.

Green Rosaries

A dark-eyed Irish beauty
at her best friend's hen party,
the local tavern where they all knew
everybody

Across the room,
her dark meet his blue—
a charmer the whole town knew,
his smile so radiant it hid
the internal battles he went through

When up, he was a good-time guy
who lit the whole pub
with his luminous energy,
she got swept right up

A smile so radiant, she forgot her pain
raised in poverty, never having enough
working herself dry
in the rural hills of the Irish countryside

A late-night mistake
in a Catholic country that didn't tolerate,
she wore baggy clothes to hide her growth
as she tried to navigate
this path alone

You see, her mother was up and down
and her gran always filled in,
she couldn't commit to a life of that again
she kept her secret from the blue-eyed charmer,
never saw him again, no one knew a thing,
except her and God

She heard of a place south of the country,
for girls out of wedlock,
packed a bag, a five-hour bus ride,
praying over her green rosaries
hoping she wasn't making
another mistake

To a convent who pretended
to have her best interests at heart
(the name itself shaming a great)
the Magdalene Laundries,
I'm sure you've seen the documentaries,
where the expectant girls in the nineteen-fifties
washed the priests' clothes,
worked like dogs in dire conditions
at a for-profit disguised as a convent,
the women isolated, imprisoned, and silent,
infants delivered by those unqualified,
and then when it was time,
the nuns signed them away
to American families

It was her name on the paperwork,
not her penmanship,
she didn't get to decide
nor say goodbye to this miracle
her body carried,
nor hello, it was over at first cry

Lies and mistreatment hidden behind a habit
their secrets covered in dark clothes,
psychological damage,
for all the babes that survived,
for all the mamas that survived
many didn't—
she was alive as was her child
for that, she felt gratitude deep inside

Yet, the dark-haired survivor never felt a loss so penetrating
her heart shattered, navigating postpartum, alone and broken,
her head spinning from the aftermath of birth,
betrayal, loss, and shame

She was determined to carry on
moving to Dublin and changing her name,
her kin could never find her though we tried
praying over our rosary beads through tears we cried

She lived in hidden anguish
never married, never had more,
kept regret deep inside,
joyless life, working herself to her core,
cleaning hotel rooms and keeping herself small
when really the dark-haired beauty
served her purpose handed to her by God—
she was the vessel to bring the family line
to the US side for all that was to come,
she fulfilled her role
yet lived in regret and sorrow,

Though I never found her on this earth
from the heavens she found me,
imparting her wisdom
telling me to move past what feels like a mistake,
to live life joyfully for what we feel holds us back
is all part of the divine plan,
but we can't see it when we're in it

She created generations
of strong, beautiful women—
change-makers, sacred creators
and though we never met
her energy is alive in me,

I've stood on her grave
watched the sky turn from storm to sun
double rainbows over her stone,
a woman of God she was
despite how dirty she was played
she never lost her faith

My grandmother from the heavens
brewing with long-held love and lessons,
she and I have always been connected
across the pond, over the wind-blown skies
by the strings of beads
from the crystal rosaries
on which we both cried.

Though We Never Met

I was always fascinated with
the story of you—
who you were and what you liked,
and if we looked alike,
the mystery of who you were,

Like a sad song that draws you in
and makes you feel heartbroken,
but it made you feel again

We walked the streets of Dublin,
toured the country on our search,
anything anyone could remember
that could serve as a clue,

Oh, how I wanted a happy reunion,
an Irish grandmother to bake me scones
and load them with jam and butter
so many I'd ruin my dinner,
who'd chat around the peat fire
and tell me about the blokes she used to date
and the pounds and pounds of potatoes
that got them through the hard winter days

I wanted connection and love
I never received growing
that I looked for in so many different ways,
the prospect of having an Irish granny
dote on me excited me to my core,
to no avail, as you had gone to heaven's door

We learned your story
the details pieced together,
divinity filling in the missing
my heart still connected to yours

Atop a mountain in your hometown
I lit a candle in the Foxford church,
dropping my coins into the wooden box
praying and watching the flame
until it would burn out,

Hours passed and the priest told me
it was time to continue on,
the flame still holding strong,
as I trod onward
leaving footprints
where you once walked

I'll always feel your light
your presence in my life,
the candle you left burning
my heart no longer seeking,
no longer yearning—
the light you left for me.

I Will Carry You Again

You've always felt connected to me,
wanting to find me so I would know you,
when *I have always known you,*
two hearts strung from the same moss
on the old oak tree

You were always seeking to find,
when your hands were empty
after your great search,
your feet standing on my grave
as you sighed

Though our eyes never met this lifetime,
we walked through the same rocky paths
the swerving pavement through the parks,
we sat on the same benches
we walked through the same doors,
we said the same prayers
we longed for something outside of us to make us whole
spending too much time yearning
for what was gone

The red parka you knew me as
holding the depths of the darkness contained in my eyes,
from the skies I watched you search for me,
now I am watching you find,
find yourself, divinity, connection, your voice
find so much more than I ever found,
as I kept myself safe and small

Be wild, be free, be strong, be brave,
all the things that make you who you are
I played the good girl, hiding who I was,
making up for my mistakes,
and it served no one

You don't have to wonder about me anymore,
you don't have to leave a trail of rosary beads
forevermore, I am with you anytime you please,
call upon my wisdom and I'll be by your side,
your grandmother in the skies,
I have love to give from where I am,
and I see no one as deserving

Receive, sweet darling, receive the love
and use it to build you back,
because you've had your challenges
just as I've had, and they have made into
who you are—
the love you have, the love you give,
the space you hold
was born from lack

Though we never met,
our DNA the same, and
a woman carries two generations
within her womb,
when you get worn, call out to me
I will carry you again.

Mama Elle

Wise beyond time,
count the wrinkles and you'll see
the mama elephant—
loving, leading, giving,
beloved matriarch

Bark off trees,
digging up roots
ivory desired by most,
communicating
through vibration
felt through the ground,
rising up to my bones
beloved matriarch

Looking back,
where was my mine?
alone, empty outlines, trying to stay close
trying to find water in the dark,
I followed you across the plains only to
end with a gaping hole in my heart

The water gone
no love or warmth
only cold, gray stone, and
you can't get water from a rock
unless your God himself

In not having,
I became what I always desired
as I can love to Sirius and back
the channels open, flowing, growing
no distance can measure
the ocean never overflows
its depth unknown

This matriarch has risen
from the puddle of muck I was given
and for so long I thought that's what I deserved
but we know what grows from the muck—
the beautiful lotus
our goddesses rest upon

It's time for me
to turn those long-carried
less-than-signs to the side
and use them to rise,
from the ground beneath,
the highest hills are layers from the past
not taking it with me but
acknowledging it for what it was
and using it to climb,

No need to keep going back—
but like the elephant
I'll never forget.

My Mother

You carried me with love in your heart,
though not the same color as the love that grew in mine,
my likeness to you is few—
but you carried me with love in your heart,
and I can hold that reverie as I continue on

Your capacity wasn't what I deserved
though for years I believed it was,
smiles, pleasantries can't make up for what isn't there to start,
my eyes widened, your line faded
at what never was

I didn't drop, nor plummet, nor spiral
instead, I was lovingly held—the Divine Mother,
Mother Gaia, ascended masters,
their lines ran deep; deep as any lineage,
threads carefully woven, their love, their compassion
carried me when your love sunk

Still afloat, my petals unfolding,
blooming from muck as the lotus does,
the Divine Mother— she holds me in her womb,
she carries me with love, as I allow in,
as I continue on, knowing
I've always been carried with love

Never without.

A Decade for Me

When my grandpa moved on,
my grandma prayed upon her rosary beads,
five decades every day—
a decade for him,
a decade for my late brother,
a decade for three more she held close,

I visited her once a month,
sitting upon her captain's chair with the braided mat,
they let her bring her favorites in,
and I listened to her stories,
her fears, as she ogled over the chocolate donuts I snuck in,

You're on my beads, she revealed,
telling me how courageous she thought me to be,
honored to be in her prayers,
honored to be seen in a way
I couldn't yet see,

Sixteen years pass,
still when a miracle appears,
when everything works out just so
I know, my grandmother's prayers
are powerfully falling from the heavens,
still in protection,
she saved the last decade for me.

Great Goddess

Sitting on the lotus
two hands up, two hands down
full of giving, even more receiving
so the cycle goes

Too often as women
we've hidden our receiving hand,
as the giving never ends
we slowly forget how
to receive

The expectation placed upon us
early in our days, that we were meant
to serve and please
to place ourselves last,
to ignore ourselves and our needs

They disempowered us
like all the greats that came before
and we let the cycle proceed

Weaved through our lives
as the care-takers and nurturers
that everyone but us deserves

After giving birth, expected to rise
and if we don't, then we're depressed
instead of taking time for our bodies to adjust

Equal roles, women in the workplace
a changing world that's not as safe,
all the tasks at home
still carrying the defaulted load
that increased exponentially
in this modern society

The kitty with the swollen eye down the road
you got her the care she needs but where is your own?
Snow White among the animals,
mothering the babes, the strangers in need,
whipping out band-aids
and cortisone creams on the beach,
but taking care of yourself doesn't feel within reach

Observing others and giving advice,
their patterns and triggers and how to move through
but your own are on the back of the stove—
forgotten like yesterday's rice,

The pretty girls on Instagram
hashing-tagging their skincare routine,
flaunting their shower as self-care
when it's a basic need

A rose in the winter
closed off and browned
waiting for spring which never came
and won't—until we learn to receive

When the flow has stopped for so long
it takes time to learn again,
the goddess upon the lotus
risen from the muck, ready and waiting
to show us—

How to receive warmth from the sun
how to receive nourishment from a cup of tea
how to receive joy from an old hobby
how to receive inner child healing swinging
from the tree, letting it fill our whole body,
from our crown to the bottoms of our feet

A blessing as we rewire,
as we remember our power
building back all the lost femineity—
the softness, the gentleness, the kindness, the love,
the flowing with the cycles of life

Giving back the hustle, the drive, the force, the nonstop
never ours to begin with
we adopted it to fit in, to keep up, to belong,
to be part of what we were excluded from
as the patriarchy saw our power
and altered our stories

So now, we rest, we receive
we slow down until we feel like speeding up
we receive the love we give,
we allow in with open hands,
it's a cycle unbroken

We feel the connection to the birds,
the trees, our hearts, the stars,
it's all one in the same,

We flow, we flow with the cycles of life,
acknowledging the beauty
of the seedlings emerging,
the flowers browning
and dropping their petals, their seeds,
each cycle honored just the same

We rest our bodies which have taken
on more than they were meant,
birthing the world,
as much as love as it brings,
it also brings pain to be healed not carried
as it can easily end up

Our goddess teaches us,
she teaches us what we were meant to be
she brings us back to ourselves
she reminds us of our intuitive ways
when our ancestors danced around maypoles,
flower ceremonies howling under the moon,
cycles synced, sisterhoods guiding,
the divine feminine rising

The love we give comes back to us,
to open up our clenched hands,
our hardened hearts
drained from the giving,
the remembering, the holding together,

Shri Lakshimi, upon the lotus
she tells us that if we open back up
that love, that compassion
will cycle right back.

Goddess Lineage

Rise, goddess, rise,
for you have spent too long
with your wings down, folded over
thinking they were broken,

When they were always whole,
waiting on your strength,
for you to understand your power,
for you to know you're connected to greater,
an invisible thread weaved across the skies
mirrored on earth through the work of the spider,

Dripping, falling, cascading water
gold veins flowing down the mountains
Quan Yin, the goddess of compassion,
with her shared lineage,
a golden tie never undone
no matter how life
has worn you down

She pours her love
and compassion to you,
from her vase of willow branches in the sky
watching your wings
fill,
unfold,
emerge,
take up space
as the color comes back in your face
wings arched, threaded through the lifetimes
as you rise, goddess, rise,
remembering all you are.

6

Stepping into Oneself

*A blank etch-a-sketch
waiting for your next drawing—
whatever will it be?*

Sunday School

"When is a gift yours?" he asked.

When you give to me.

As the words left her lips, she knew that didn't sound right.

The bell rang, and his voice heightened to be heard over the noise:

A gift is yours when you receive it.

She heard him, but it took many years to receive the message—and the abundance that came after.

The Power of Writing

Writing these verses, these rhymes,
these feelings from deep inside
freeing me from what I held
through the written word
rising
heart to mind
fingers typing
creating while breaking
fences, barriers all down
in destruction there's creation
more room, more spacing,
a beautiful heart-opening powerfully radiating
as I watch what held me down
turn to gold
in deep transformation.

Living Bigger

I could be living bigger
instead of staying small,
I tiptoe, eyes down,
trying not to be a bother,
trying not to make a sound,
hiding parts of who I am,
uncovered only in places
where I won't be the only one

Welded to the language of limits,
beliefs that were yours, not mine
but when roads merged
I took everything on—
stories I told myself
to keep me safe when I was young,
but she is not me, she is gone,

I could be living bigger
instead of playing safe
throwing numbers into excel,
quantifying what can only be felt,
hanging onto what no longer fit
because the tally added up

Swimming in circles in a bowl
when the ocean was in front of me,
holding on to what isn't mine,
things stuck to me for so long
convinced they were character flaws,
but no, they didn't belong

I could be living bigger
using my true voice,
not the high-pitched people-pleaser
nor the growl of giving orders,

but one rooted in my heart,
where the words I choose
don't need to be unraveled,
as the energy within comes
through its channel

And I see myself—
a miniature statue on the nightstand
turning circles, music playing
as she goes round and round,
not realizing, the cover is gone

New avenues that don't go in circles,
room to grow, limits not made of glass,
I can keep the glitter and
make my own path
I am not the same,
my place in this world changed,
everything led me here
yet like before, I'm still playing small,
trying to hide my presence
erasing my footprints in the sand,
leaving everything as it was

And a voice comes,
you weren't meant to leave everything as it was
it could never be that way again,
because of you, your presence
the light and love and joy you bring—
why would you try to be one twinkling light
when you are the whole string, the whole sky,
bringing magic and sparkles
to the room, the night, the lives of those around,
do not try to be anything other than what you are
nor anything less—you, at your fullest

If everyone lived in their true form,
what a beautiful world this would be
the one that the greats dreamed of,
the true age of love
golden as can be

You're one tiny person in a large universe
but when you're living in your light,
the grand design, you feel completely aligned
and others start finding the places they shine

And now I know, I'm living exactly as I'm meant
in love, in joy, not dimming my light
in realization of who I was, who I am,
how I stayed small to keep me safe
but now I have the tools, the space,
to really step into who I'm meant to be
living in true authenticity
out of the bowl, I jump
wild and free.

This Comfy Space

Can I stay here? she said curiously.

No, you're meant for far bigger things.

She nodded and started moving along.

Armor

The swords are down, the fight is gone
the tears return after being locked for so long,
pouring out with no rhythm, or flow, or cadence
flooding the eyes, no tissue to catch,
no sleeve to hide behind,

Letting them flow and run as water is meant
down her cheekbones in drips and drops,
her face glazed, in disarray she looks
through the enamored mask,
puffy, shiny, drooping eyes,

All of this was held inside, now surfacing and healing
though it doesn't feel good, better out than in,
she can't keep and store all the old emotion,
letting it puddle underneath the swords
she had long been holding,

Medieval plates and cups lined across the wooden table,
where the knight drinks ale from her silver cup
Who's to tell her the fight is over?
Who's to tell her it's okay to cry?
Who's to tell the knight that her reflection in the silver
is only a disguise,
as all she is, is held behind?

Sliding off the armor
laying it next to the swords,
not to be preserved, but transmuted
into a softer container she can hold herself in,

The fight is gone, the tears wash away all that was,
flooding out the mud that kept her feet heavy and stuck,

Back to water, back to dirt,
and in time, the ground will dry
grass will grow in that space again,
without the armor, without the old stories
from the tears she cried.

Realign with Self Era

I'm in my realign-with-self era,
where I pour poetry onto the burning candle at 3am
setting fire to what's-brewing-inside-of-me era,

As I release the darkness and depth
that I always felt behind your kind words, your faux smiles,
where your eyes never matched what I felt
where I broke contact era

Desperately on purpose
after taking on what wasn't mine era,
where I gave you my worth to hold in your hands
to which you slammed on the table,
remnants of my worth splattered—

The not-no-more era, where I don't stand so small
where I don't give out everything I have,
where I realize I can stretch and pull myself up to a new place
the learn-to-walk-again era

Where I find my footing without your criticisms,
your I-know-best mentality hovering over me
as I walk the wide-open galleries
looking for freedom in paintings
cause I couldn't find it inside of me era,

Where the shadow doesn't fall behind me,
nor in front of me, nor side-to-side
but seamlessly integrated as part-of-me era,

Where I work through what I long-carried
instead of turning my head era

I'm in my love-myself era,
where I realize your capacity to love
had nothing to do with me,

I'm in the trust-myself era
where no one, no man can silence or question
the intuition flowing through this sacred soul era,

I'm in my turn-pain-to-gold era,
where I align with my inner alchemist,
learning the laws of the universe,
the lessons of nature and connecting to greater for which I am era

I'm in my creation era,
where I pull emotions through creative channels,
keys I tap on the old upright piano,
strings of words flowing out as healing pours in,

I'm in the letting-my-voice-bring-healing era,
where I am no longer in hiding trying to contain all I feel,
all I've been through era

I'm in my realign-with-self era,
where I pour poetry onto the burning candle at 3am,
setting fire to what's-no-longer-brewing-inside-of-me era.

Mold

You were on my radar ages ago
the heartbreak and turmoil and destructive power
you held was one I knew all too well,
never up-close but enough knowledge held in my hands
to spark my intuition, a tiny flame easily ignored
and let's call that lesson one—
not listening to myself

I knew about you before I encountered you,
it couldn't be, I said more than once
as I had done my due diligence,
this couldn't happen to us, my system too sensitive,
it doesn't track I told myself as I tried to sleep,
the detective in me running scripts of this puzzle I couldn't crack,
runny noses and chronic illness triggered
with no explanation other than the four walls of this house,
air filters turning red, the smell of burnt toast that spread,
a gray cloud hovering, windows open,
humid air all leading to the grand uncovering,
and he, he dismissed me when I told him my fear,
silencing my concerns over the heavy air,
we were on the same team but not working together
a colossal mess, a game of musical chairs,
yet there was no winner, an unhealthy dynamic
that played out for far too long,
but when only one person can see it,
how do you convince yourself it's real?
no longer sustainable, empty, vacant
excavating the junk we had dragged around for years
a dumpster filled with more than we knew we held,
twice the work, twice the pain, constant tears
I turn my volume up to be heard, this time too loud,
the radio blaring when you start your car,
noise so intense you don't hear the words
falling onto the hard ground,
short-circuiting instead of connecting
stuck in the same level of the video game,
unable to jump to the next rock to move us forward
repeating the level over and over but no real progress made,
let's call this lesson two: the video game

When you place a drop of water in a microscope,
you see miracles in the crystalline formations
but when water has long been stagnant
seeping into places it was never meant,
one way in, no way out
the crystalline structure rearranges,
depictions of love and compassion no longer,
vapid growth of what doesn't belong,
a relationship born out of love and compassion grown stale,
no great flood, no massive destruction
but small holes, cracks in the foundation
and that was enough to wreak havoc on what was,
never fixed, never acknowledged, never any action
except water puddling behind the scenes,
a blank stare as you say, coughing from the languid air,
everything looks fine to me
and I react as I always do—not positively
stuck on the same step, reflecting you, reflecting me
and here we are on the mirror of lesson three

Water thousands and thousands of years old
holding the akashic records within its molecules,
pooled under the baseboard, within the wall,
now stuck, stagnant, no longer flowing
so long-ignored that symptoms and sickness arise
from the darkness within these walls,
but the wolves are back in Yellowstone
the light is here again,
to bring back the ecosystem
that even mold has a place in,
to restore what was, but before we do,
accepting the mayhem that came before,
how the wolves served their purpose,
as challenging as the turmoil was,
the unsafety and fear that left me defeated,
my nervous system crashed, depleted
as each door revealed more and more
still, for my feet to be standing where they are
my heart holds gratitude for lesson four

We all love stories
even ones that no longer serves our bodies,
as humans, we keep repeating and repeating
keeping ourselves drenched in the rain,
umbrella inside out, ankle-deep sloshing in water
when we can just step out
as hard as it is to face,
knowing the emotion is valid
yet the experience has changed,
the way it plays out makes us feel the same,
what once kept us safe—patterns that protected
our former self no longer serve,
our trauma to acknowledge and release,
with lesson five here to show the relation,
old and new wounds overlapping, intersecting
with a grand revelation:
water, just like feelings, is meant to flow—it's vital,
there's no stagnancy in the water cycle,
second grade science, holding secrets for the soul
on how to move forward
that kept-emotions are suppressed symptoms
our bodies hold the memories, just as the water does,
as lesson six is one of validating all the feelings needing feeling,
not capped or trapped within the streaked ceiling

And so, we discover where the water stopped flowing
and we clean and cleanse and clear and create new,
we strengthen and brighten and deepen
and we make it to the next rock, to the next level
our skills are greater, our capacity wider,
our bodies stronger, our hands interlocked,
love and compassion here again

Letting the water *flow* and *destruct*
and *create* and *transform* and *change*
letting the relationship evolve and cycle— not stay the same
letting the emotions be felt and go on their way
letting the past versions of myself know *this is not that,* she is safe
And know, that stagnancy, in any form, doesn't serve anybody
it only causes mold to grow.

The Empath's Return

Last night I dreamt of him and her
a decade together ending,
an elegant party marking their split

Yet, he and she had smiles
plastered across their faces,
oddly enough, everyone did

Except for me
an emotional wreck,
my tears were streaming

Why are you crying? a stranger asked,
Do you even know them?
How does it affect you?

I can feel his heartbreak

Heartbreak? He's smiling,
the stranger responds

Smile or not,
I feel others' emotions
as deeply as my own
his overarching sadness
enveloped me

A lifetime I've had of taking on and stuffing down
large emotions—some were mine,
some were not

A lifetime of not listening to my inner guidance,
believing the false smiles,
and landing flat on my face

A lifetime of beliefs that I was weak,
foolish, emotional, everything the
patriarchy tries to paint women like me

It was time to fully embrace myself—
this gift, using my divine perception and
intuition as powerful guidance they've always been

With gratitude for this gift, this awareness,
I send back to him what isn't mine to carry,
along with a little love to help him along

I watch as his smile starts to fade,
tears collect, and he reveals his sadness,
his heartbreak—
his to experience and release

The color in my face returns,
as I wipe the last of my tears
collecting myself, blessing my gift,
grateful for the step forward

In our dreams, we wake.

Higher Self

I am the light of the stars,
your true essence intact,
holding you while you're on earth
and trying to tap in,
as much as you are willing.

Squeaky Floor

As you swing back and forth, your foot pushes the floor,
the squeak between the boards takes you straight back
to the times you sat in the blue-cushioned rocking chair,
each forward movement squeaking the floor,
again and again, never fixed, until you left

Into a safe space, the shaggy red rug no longer at your feet
absorbing, holding onto everything,
the paneled walls down, room for you to grow
light pouring through the windows
love, leaves, empty space, trees

Yet returning to that part of yourself
where you tiptoed around others,
deciphering their expressions
like a secret code, that only you knew
the key to survival

Where *I love yous* were thrown, not even watered down,
instead of feeling soft and fuzzy, they were the twig you
snapped with your foot—
broken but not split

When everything seemed like it didn't fit—
hand-me-downs too baggy, too long,
too drab, dark, losing yourself in costumes
until you saved ten dollars and bought a shirt at 579,
and felt like a queen, the words you heard,
the lack of feelings showed,
that ten-dollar shirt with its burgundy stripes
was the start of you stepping out on your own,
feeling what fit and what didn't

Reading the room, the expressions you knew
seeing how you were received

and how you weren't,
taking it too hard like you had before,
trying to fit into a copper mold on the wall until it dropped,
with your heart as it sunk to the floor,
the grief of loss overwhelming your life when you
thought you finally had it figured out

And then learning again how to survive without,
all the places rearranged, no order, no logic remained,
a view covered in fog—dense, cold
everyday overcast even when there was sun,
when your companions were the smoke filling the night sky,
alone you trekked seeing your breath in the cold,
the lonely stars above, the bottom of the bottle,
burnt tacos, sleep when you could
waiting tables, taking orders
serving others to deflect—
apron tied, dark eyes, sullen face,
feeling lost and hopeless,

Before you hit the ground
the universe threw you a star
to love you in a way no one had,
and together you took up space in the dark sky,
to have him by your side
to feel love as unconditional,
for the first time in your whole life is why you cried
in happiness, in sadness, in fear of repeat
when you have something you never want to lose
you hold too tight, letting the future set the pace,
your dreams spaced, out of reach
but the prospect of having dreams again felt great

You had no tools, nothing at all—
now you have a bucket, a bench, a garage,
a shed, filled with so many things to draw upon, but not then
all you had was him, and that was enough,

until you watched your dreams float by,
when you reached you fell out of the sky,
and back to the ground
realizing they weren't shared
and this time when you landed flat,
you weren't at the bottom of the hole,
but stable ground, easier to stand
your heart was broken, more walls went up,
but you were happy to have been loved

Building back with the few things you had
a life you were proud of,
trying different grounds and seeing how you stood
how far you came, picking what worked, leaving what didn't
you wished to walk alone again,
but you were met with love,
two stars tethered creating space
where you could both reach your dreams
from where you were, without condition, without reason
a tough thing to wrap your weathered mind around

And you built your life, a beautiful one
your eyes glistened again,
each chamber of your heart filled
even the ones locked,
the story, the path you longed for,
and in your childhood imagination, it ends there
when the girl finds love and opens her heart again

Yet just the beginning of all you went through,
the start of your work together and solo
more lessons, the universe had been waiting on,
resuming after the pause, to move you forward,
a different trajectory, with more tools acquired,
so when it all shattered again, as it did,
you got through with more ease than before

Though the biggest difference made
when you turned your face to the heavens
and watched your path change,
you found connection again—
the sun shining on your skin
another star to hold you
in pure divinity
when the sky fell

Your path zigzags
yet all the parts fit, every last piece
the lines drawn in the sky,
stopping at different highlights
needing someone to love you
to pick you up again, but then
you were strong enough on your own to navigate
and get through without depending on,
where your partner wasn't a rescuer
nor a tow truck on the lonely road,
nor an extension of you,
but rather gentle support
as life moves you both forward

The tools you have now take up space,
you take up space,
no longer cowered in the corner
turning down your own feelings
in hand-me-downs, reading faces,
instead finding strength in your voice,
your story, yourself

And as you sit and swing back and forth,
your son calls your name,
your foot goes to stop the swing
reaching for the squeak in the floor that
started the recollecting,
as your foot taps around

there's no squeak to be found,
as the reminiscence
released the tension
of what was stuck

Your story now on the page
with all the emotions that came,
even with the pain, the hurt, the late start,
all the figuring out, the shadows of grief,
the absence of love so early in life,
if you peer between the branches of pain
you'll find hidden gifts,
glimmers of light waiting
yours to discover
like the moss sprinkled on the old oak trees,
covered in blessings
but first comes acceptance,
compassion, forgiveness
for yourself
and all that came before,
because all that pain and sadness
made you who you are,
the strong, resilient,
compassionate,
empowered
angelic
presence
that stands forth.

Did You Know?

Did you know I'm an open book but a mystery at the same time, you don't know which page to turn to or what timeline?

Did you know I'm soft, so very soft, and if I have to harden into the masculine I crack?

Did you know the love my heart holds can be felt by those who can't feel anything else? But I have trouble with that, as I take their words for what their worth when their heart doesn't match

Then I'm in conflict and judgment of myself, for I can't place what doesn't feel right so I just go along?

Felt time and time again, when will I learn my lesson? Did you know I internalize my emotion, I'm still learning how to not store it

Did you know I still carry wounds from feeling unseen?
a trigger from my childhood days, a family of seven,
the easy one who slides right by, vying to be seen, to be loved
reprimanded for wanting attention, be the good girl, be quiet, smile,
follow along—ducks in a row, all a narcissistic show

Did you know I find healing hard, that I feel worn so many days, that I'm in overwhelm of all I signed up for this lifetime?

It feels like standing on the high dive when I was a kid, no more than five, I stood as the board wiggled, and I inched out, as the lifeguards cheered

Did you know I didn't jump? I turned around, walked down the ladder and that's the day I began living small

Did you know that I made a promise with the Universe
that I would live large, but I can't remember making it,
and a little mad at myself for it, I just want to float on a raft
with cucumbers over my eyes, the warm sun beating down

Did you know the Universe whispers me secrets?
She told me to live in moments, that I can have my raft moment,
but first I must return to the high dive.

Wheels of Energy

When out of balance,
lean into the gust without getting knocked down,
grounding yourself inward
one level up, one down

It all connects—
thousands of constellations in the sky
thousands of wheels of energy
flowing through, the lines of the rainbow
a walk-through gallery of you

An opportunity to see
what needs shining or straightening
finding the disconnect,
for when you strengthen one
they all flow more freely,
balancing you in a way you can't see,
but you can feel, if you soften the senses you've
known all your life, and lean into the energy of
what's beyond.

Within Myself

Sometimes I forget who I am
I forget that I am divine and not ego,
I'm not this fragile human needing to be built up
or my inner child reliving old stories

I am a divine force of love and light,
an extension of the stars themselves

I have what I need within myself.

Showers of Love

Shower me with the waters of forgiveness
so that I may move on,
let it flow through me, around me
so my mind can settle down,
so my heart can connect
to the glistening rays of forgiveness
knowing I'm perfect the way I am

Shower me with the waters of compassion
toward myself because I've spent my life
giving but not receiving back,
let it grow up through the ground
a tulip from its bulb
my toes grounded in the dirt from its growth,
so I'm always reminded to give compassion to myself

Shower me with the waters of love
so that I can return to all the old versions of me
and tell her she is loved, even in situations where she felt none,
to remind her she was never alone, even though love was taught
to her in a different way than most,
love always existed where she did,
but she had to feel it first

Shower me with the waters of gratitude
so I feel in every cell, every atom,
how amazing it is to be here and to be loved,
to be walking with those beside me
who expand my heart wider, fuller, flowing,
knocking down the walls of sand and dirt,
connecting the waters of gratitude with the flow of my heart,
the most beautiful fountain that never turns off

Shower me with the waters of joy,
the colors of the rainbow, the brightest of all shades
reminding me of the happiness in every moment,
our eyes the most beautiful filter,
finding the joy to make everything brighter

Shower me with goodness, to wash away all that isn't,
anything stuck, anything holding me back,
anything I don't need to carry,
all the times my compassion wasn't detached,
shower me with the waters of goodness to clean and bring in,
like the powerful river—clearing and creating all in one swig

And then, I'll thank divinity for the glorious rainfall
connecting to the extraordinary powers of the water.

Full Self

When you're afraid of being your full self,
so you let a fraction seep through
like light peering through the limbs
gentle and soft but not full strength,
secondhand light dances between branches
you become more comfortable with who you are
letting more and more shine through
until the tree you've hid behind is gone,
you're full sun, shining like you've never before
not dimming, not dimming again
for anyone.

The First Time I Felt Peace

Laying in Savasana
on the concrete riverwalk
gentle lapping of waves on both sides
the sun sinking into a fiery orange sky

My body relaxed, as I felt strong
and powerful for the first time,
defying the beliefs I held as true in my mind
I had moved with my breath,
followed along, taking in all
I thought I wasn't capable of

With nature holding me
providing the most beautiful show,
watching the unimaginable unfold
silhouettes of dolphins in the distance
as my limited beliefs untwisted

And once in a yellow moon
a majestic bagpiper would show,
filling the air with his beautiful notes
I was lost, but now I'm found
echoing through my soul

Each week I return to feel that way again
to refill my body, to restore my soul
tears of gratitude stream,
my brokenness quiets
I am whole

The beauty of nature, an amazing teacher,
a mind ready to rewire all coming together
to form magic on the outside,
reflecting what already existed inside

Igniting a light that I could now see,
the magic in me when I allowed myself
for the first time to just be,
and finally, I felt peace.

Life in Shapes

The artist churning out shapes—
circles upon circles, the wheels of the bicycle,
larger and smaller,
lines connecting, intersecting
creating cones, cylinders, polygons
in what looks to be a beautiful collage
of sacred geometry,
parallels shown in perfect transparency

We are little colored dots moving along
different paths laid out,
free will involved,
higher and lower tracks
choices, paths, it's all displayed—
yet there's also space for newness created
the canvas full and empty simultaneously,
an optical illusion of various degrees
showing how one can ascend higher and bolder and brighter
than this geometric canvas of color,
if the dot can stop itself from going round the same circles
as they are cycles we keep repeating
not realizing they are meant to end
for something greater,

Through the eyes of old Dutch painter—
life in shapes.

Deeper

The young girl at the door
smiling as if she owned the world,
only letting a few in
she waved on those
who understood her depths,
nothing surface level here exists

Once inside
the melodies arrived,
pipe dreams and their possibilities,
deepest fears, epiphanies,
hats and coats checked
no facades here

An ocean for her to explore,
which way to go when there's
so much to absorb?
smiling at memories
rooted in the heart,
a stark contrast to before
thinking back to her elders and those
who never really knew her,
appearance-based
the little brown shopping bag
pretty, smart, loading on the
compliments before the grand smear,
it didn't go deeper than it appeared

She's made of stardust through God's design,
but if you only skim the surface
all you'll find is dust,
not realizing it's made
from stars

Those she allowed in
recognizing the same in them,
safe to share her heart—
all the colors of the rainbow
not just the ones they wanted to see,
each and every color in all its majestic glory

And if you gather them all together
for a round of *Galway Girls,*
all the occupations that came before,
the easy walks that didn't fit,
shifting the sorrow, a gift reframed
wrapped in shimmering paper,
they'd nod in knowingness, saying,
Good on her, cheering as if nothing
made more sense in the world

And she'd smile knowing she is back on the path
honoring herself, aligned with the gulfs of
who she was before, who she still is
the path she started long ago
but trailed off—for milestones,
people-pleasing, the ego

Artsy pictures on the wall,
feathers hanging from her ears
gallery walks, creative sparks wherever she goes,
and that outlet for the depth of her to show
taking pain, moving through, shifting,
into this book of pure magic,
showing she was never into
surface level sh*t.

Earth School

How do you learn to step into your power again, after a lifetime of
handing it out, there for the taking but not anymore?

How do you learn to trust yourself, to access the healing
power within your body, your soul, a portal to so much more?

How do you learn to realign yourself, in those moments of
disconnect, to the frequency of love to which you are?

How do you shed the old patterns, deeply engrained in your DNA,
carried through the generations, covered wagons trailing across the
states, the vehicles changed but the pattern remains?

How do you let go of the fears taking up space in your mind,
your ego protecting you, running reels of fears in the background
keeping you out of the present moment and lost in the unknown?

How do you soften after a lifetime of being tough, dropping the
hustle, the force, the masculine that your feminine never
had a place in?

How do you hop to a higher timeline when you realize the low road
no longer serves?

How do you start again from nothing, the bottom of the barrel,
dirt-stained toes, building again, this time different than before?

How do you retire the old stories playing on repeat, swirling
through your mind, across timelines, coming in different forms to
be healed but how?

How do you know what's next, when to pivot or when to keep going,
when to push on, when to rest, which choices are best?

How do you unlearn what you thought was truth? How do you walk
softer? How do you love deeper? How do you prioritize self?

Lessons never tackled in the classroom, no notes, no powerpoint,
but if you squint up at the sky on a clear night,
you'll see the scrolls held in the light of the stars
and maybe find some answers for your time at earth school.

Let the Goodness In

Keep-a-going, the train keeps moving,
no looking back, you are already past that,
pushing through the landscape
blazing a trail that's never been before

When the doubts emerge, let them dissolve into
the most beautiful clouds and continue on their way
as you continue on yours

Exciting and scary simultaneously, the excitement
dominates, as the scene around the corner is more beautiful
than the one in your mind

Filled with new possibilities, places and people and things—
goats on a field of pine trees helping you rewrite old stories,
an artist on the cobblestone streets painting you as you see yourself,
the most enchanting village you've ever stumbled upon,
you never want to leave

Ascended masters looking upon the town
their love lighting it up as it seeps into your heart,
you are in awe of how all this exists
it always has, but you were bound
by the limits in your mind

Keep-a-going, onward, upward, forward
doing the work, learning the lessons
living in joy, in love, in light and surrendering to all of life

Let the goodness in, not just seep through the cracks
not condensation on the cold window pane
a wide open door, wide open heart
let the goodness in
to finally be enjoyed.

Light Language

Tethered to the Swiss diver
I jump out of the helicopter,
frozen in awe after the freefall,
he speaks in English, I don't respond
he tries again—Spanish, French, German, Swiss,
before falling back to English
what language do you speak?
his voice inching toward frustration,
background noise to me

In my dreamy state
feeling only peace, gently drifting
through whispering mountain peaks
I defy gravity restoring ethereal memories,
I've been before and will again
a dimension I know well
my body remembering

Where birds dropped bundles of light
and goodness in a glimmer of dew,
where souls go to learn
their lessons, to study, to grow
meeting in love, in joy, and light,
where the stars hold your soul and
any sparkles that fell off are given right back,
where my children chose me in pure
knowingness of the magic we'd create,
where this soul of mine knew only light,
deeply connected to the stars
journeying across the clouds,
humbled treetops canopied in love

The civilizations that came before
the lightworkers and light bodies that returned,
where I danced with my ancestors in pure delight
where I knew my guardian angel inside and out
where my pups wait for me to see again
after guiding me through this life,
where the trolley patiently rolls on
round and round like the lessons of our time,

A world long-hidden in an antique set of drawers
like an old set of pearls passed across the line
guarded by the grandmothers,
holding coveted magic like the horn of the unicorn

He taps my shoulder
no longer could I ignore,
teach me the language you speak
he says with more compassion than before
I respond,
metaphors,
I speak in metaphors
he nodded, he knew
he was in receipt
of the golden set of doors
he opened for me.

Saturn

Swinging from the rings of Saturn
my fairy tales come alive
as I find my way back to who I've always been

Surrounded by deep blues seeping into purples
showing the evolution of my soul

Memories drift covered in glimmers of gold stardust
as if projected, though nothing was ever more real

Here in space, I'm boundless, flowing, free
effortlessly gliding with the universe's breath
as I swing amidst the stars.

Red Camaro in the Sky

I'm here when you need
you can connect anytime you please,
we are still together
our journeys running parallel,
different dimensions if you will
but still side-by-side
traveling together after all this time

I am here
wisdom to share
space to hold
loving words to give
I could never forget you,
my journey moves with you,
don't dwell in what has passed
let these now moments replace what was

You are never alone
I am right beside
in the throes of being human
there's more than meets the eye,
so lean on me when you need
my silhouetted shoulder waiting,
rest your head and let me drive
the red Camaro through the night sky,
following the trail of dust drifting from the stars
letting the cool air relieve your scars

One hand on the wheel
one wrapped around you,
reminiscent of the power wheels
we rode when we were young,
pedal to the ground
as you trusted me
my sidekick at only three,
I protected you then,
I will again

Count the stars as if they were sheep
letting your eyes gently close
knowing you are safe,
rest in this loving space I hold,
the wonders of the universe
watching your journey unfold
as I take the wheel for a while
and you rest in knowingness
that you are safe, supported, and loved—

On we roll
into the night within,
eight-cylinder to the wind.

Your Strength

When I hear your story
your voice wavering
as it meets the hazy air,
pain radiating,
I sit in awe

In awe of your
strength and resilience,
of how you got through,
how much you stretched when others
would have fallen apart,
in awe of how you are able to move on
in grace and love and joy,
learning from the past, the missteps
learning how you can safely trust
learning how to step into yourself,
I sit in awe of you

Wishing you could see
how amazing you are.

The Artist Across

On the streets of Florence,
there was an artist wearing a black beret,
he steered the boats in Venice
until the motion made him sick,

Knowing flat ground is where he needed to be
he turned his paddle to a brush,
to paint all that he saw, all he felt
using the water in a different way
flowing into this new state,

Deeply connected to his paints,
the water, his heart, his paddle now laid,
he sat on his stool on the cobblestone streets
painting the scenes he lived through,
the favorite on the street, the tourists would gawk,
the locals brought chocolates and fruit
and his Leo moon would inflate,
like a balloon, tied to the chair
so it didn't float away

But deep down, he felt mediocre,
he had too late a start
always comparing to everyone else
finding their gifts but not acknowledging his,
his shadow not quite right, the tree branch looks off,
his inner dialogue always picking apart

You might not paint a perfect shadow
or hit a note exactly as so,
but the love you pour in
is the most beautiful art,

A sacred creator he was,
you are, from the start
it's not the talent that comes through
but one's connection to their heart

You see, it doesn't span one lifetime
nor one dimension, but all of those your soul
has been a part of—an artist in one, a writer in
another, musician, carpenter, baker,
all sacred creators

The art is woven through every lifetime you've had,
as you unwrap those gifts in each existence that comes after,
you are awakening the art from another
lining your path with creation
not separate from who you are,
all intertwined into a series of many lifetimes

When you pick up the brush, or the pen, or the guitar,
you are picking up where you left off in another.

Soul's Gold

An old book you had written in
penning a dream you had since forgotten—
as if writing to your future self,
messages that can only be felt
serving as a beautiful reminder
of the past and present aligning,
dots connect, goodness unfolds
when you follow what was always meant—your soul's gold.

Be Still

Sometimes I lay in bed
not in sickness or symptoms
not in laziness, not ignoring
yet resting and integrating
all that I am now,
leaving all that was
a gentle and slow process,
letting what comes surface,
tears seep with sadness,
forgiveness

Tears pour in pride, honoring all
I have been through, obstacles lined
as I conquered the hill
tearing the ribbon this time,
hands clapping, angels cheering
for me and my journey,
for the ability to reflect and renew,
my nervous system heals
from all it's been through,
turning from the hustle,
the mindless tasks, now
integrating, circulating
separated from what
was frustrating,
I am still,
for the first time
in my life, my God,
I am still.

Honoring It All

There's a place for hard, for messy, for brokenness
There's a place for acceptance, stillness, acknowledgment

There's a place for motion, moving forward, letting go
There's a place for ease, for growth

The magic comes from honoring all the parts of the cycle
instead of trying to control or will away

Honor where you are in each moment of each day.

Undefinable

A role, a job, a title is not all there is to me,
just a small piece of who I am
I can be something
without that something defining me.

Symphony of Light

A symphony of rising and falling, connecting, uniting,
sound within the human experience,
as the notes harmonize, the bell chimes,
connecting parts of our lives,
sounds of the ocean, soothing, softening,
the deep-rooted gong, clearing, releasing
the reciprocity of giving and receiving,
light in creation, circulation, magnification

As the story is told of two connecting,
the ripples sent out from across the pond,
everything that had to occur previously
for this one moment, orchestrated by the Divine
for the magic to unfold, to reach further,
to provide the next stone in reaching their soul's gold
and receiving blessings—divine siblings meeting
helping, guiding, loving, the bowls singing, the pen writing
hands playing, fingers typing,
divinity in creation, layers of manifestation
in reaching wider with their gifts
connected by the Divine Mother
in beautiful purpose

Each of our single existences serves much greater,
strings once tangled, now woven together
to form a magnificent tapestry,
each thread holds together its radiant beauty

My mind unwinding at all it thought it knew
now beginning to understand the formless
and the lines she no longer drew,
a symphony of sound, of verses reaching greater
rooted in strength, in laughter while our souls smile knowing
the divine ripples will keep spreading about
to love, laugh, live, and create as we were meant,
letting it fill us up—as our light widens and circles out.

My Life, My Light

I'll carry the torch now
thank you for grasping it when I stumbled
so the oil wouldn't spill across my feet

Thank you for holding it higher than my arms could go,
illuminating my landscape so I wouldn't scare in twilight

When the flame went out, leaving me in the grimmest of nights,
thank you for reigniting my torch with patience and love

Yet, I keep looking to you to shine,
searching outside of myself,
seeking clarity and answers externally,
panicking over being in the darkness, in my fears, in the ashes

While grateful to you for carrying my torch,
it's long time I carried it myself
knowing everything I need is within,
time for me to learn how to be in my power,
how to carry my own light,
how to shine in a way where my landscape is complete

I might burn my feet
I might trip in the shadows
yet I will hold faith in myself

I can balance across this beam
I'm on this earth to do greater,
I've watched my own mistakes
I've watched myself give my power away
I've watched myself diminish my accomplishments
chalking them up to someone else's kindness

My hands are shaking as I reach out
yet if I want to move forward,
it's time to carry my own light
in a way I haven't yet.

The Essence of Becoming

The way a potter places his sculpture in the kiln
ramped up thousands of degrees
burning its very essence
never again will it be the same,

And what's left when the fire is gone,
the embers are out
after the pain and the grief and the hardship
when we feel burnt to a crisp—

A perfect piece of art,
shiny and glazed with a sparkle that couldn't yet exist
that only became what it is
because of the heat it endured,
an intensity you wouldn't wish
left you with a beautiful gift.

7

Connecting to Nature & Greater

*Miracles surround
you're connected to greater—
oneness in nature.*

Tuning In

Settled leaves
from when the wind quieted
crunch beneath my feet
as they line my path
through the woods

Blanketing the earth
guiding the way out—
toward the light of the canal

Crossing the barn red bridge
as it held my footsteps with grace,
for my contemplative moments
for the sadness that came
for the comfort when displaced

To the water—
was the message,
though barriers blocked its flow
the water was freedom,
stagnant and all

In summer, amidst the heat,
panting dogs unleashed
jumping in to cool off

In autumn, red and orange
leaves dropped for a dip
before they browned

In winter, skaters emerged,
carefully coasting out, the perfect
snowy setting for a rom-com

But spring, spring was
the loveliest of all—as the wildflowers
framed this magical space
with new beginnings in tow

Drawn to this beautiful escape,
a spot to clear my mind,
an easy bike ride, a shortcut to town,
a place to go when I had none,
memories, emotions including heavy ones,
along the towpath of the canal

As I sat on a grassy hill
watching, taking in, enjoying
this water that never seemed to move
the locks and dams blocking its path,
though the water adapted to the seasons
there was never forward flow

And my eyes widen in discovery—
this water was me, so many beautiful parts
in all her seasons, but stuck in stagnancy

Walls surrounded me, I adapted as best I could
but the locks remained, blocking my path,
no forward movement made

While this place recharged me, balanced me, held space for me,
it was time to take its lessons and move on
as I needed space to flow to bigger things,
that I can take the beauty that surrounds me,
that is me, and safely move on
without the locks and dams stopping me,
natural, in flow, as water is meant to be

We are so quick to take advice from a friend,
to people-please our path, but when was the last time
we received guidance from the natural world that
surrounds—a bird, a tree, an old canal,
wisdom quietly waiting for us to dial in

When we get quiet within ourselves,
tuning in to our surroundings,
there are lessons and messages to which
we are naturally connected,
as we are made from what's around us—
the places, the plants, the animals, the mountains,
the moon cycles, the sunrises that we are drawn to,

We are nature
all the same divine creator,
holding their wisdom in hand
waiting for us to receive,
as they guide us to the next season
helping us flow forward,
when we welcome in the
messages of the natural world
to which we have always been a part of.

Winding Roads

I drove past a field of cows
quite slow so I could tell them hello,
as I rolled down my window,
I heard, "Thank you for your light,"
my eyes filled with tears
as I nodded in receipt
and thanked them for theirs.

Half-Moon

The half-moon shining down, illuminating the embers of my soul,
wherein lies the disconnect between the waters and me?
never feeling strong in my body, the tears that never come,
leaking emotions instead of feeling, thrown by the ocean herself,
lacking the ability to flow with the cycles
not knowing how to work with the water—

Learning how to float, how to flow, how to be,
no longer fighting, ignoring nor resisting
surrendering, strengthening, understanding
the powerful force of water is also in me,
in connection to the elements
that make up my mind, my soul, my body—

I am the ocean and it is me.

Surrender

In the way the wind blows the branches
and all that isn't for me flutters away

Browned, crunched leaves barely hanging on,
now air-bound, a beautiful shower as
they twist, twirl, flutter, float
landing softly, gently on the dirt

And my tree has space, capacity,
for new growth in its place

The wind took what was ready to go—
a timely release.

Light Beings in the Magical Forest

You asked what I did today
I sat amongst the trees
in a space I felt safe
and I received,
their magic, their blessings,
their quiet strength

So many pass by without really knowing
not me, not anymore, the soft strength of the trees
is where my heart called me today
with its gentle gifts to bestow,
I soak in their wisdom before I carry on

Each tree with stories to share,
their cavernous roots forging into the earth
their branches, hands opening to the heavens in receipt,
carrying messages sourced by divinity,
if you can hear their whispers as you walk this earth,
how similar we are to the tree

I ground myself on Mother Gaia's bench,
resetting my clock, allowing in, recentering,
connecting me back when my body forgot

If I were one of these trees, I'd be the old oak
that's been there forever, there for you to depend on
deep-rooted, kind wisdom, still growing

The moss are sprinkles of divinity
draped over the branches of the old tree,
all the times I felt stuck, more sprinkled on
reminding me of my magic

Each new branch curving outward as if it's falling,
the next direction, yet I get scared when I can't see,
the curves were dead-ends previously, where the limb
broke off, the path I was on when it all fell apart,
yet there are more limbs growing, do I focus
on the brokenness, or the new growth?

Hopping over to a new path
I want to take the one that goes up,
toward the heavens so I'll always remember
but the slant is high and it looks tough,
it's all part of my growth, I suppose,
staying the same never worked for me
nor the old oak tree

Little eyes appear with gray fur all around
from behind me, the oak tree,
as if hiding or seeking, one can't tell,
I watch a man look at me in awe as I talk
to the squirrel who stopped in front of my foot,
interacting species in trust

And then, feathers of blue glide by
landing silently by my side, and I break
into tears, you and I both know
that blue jay is you, like you he flew away too quick,
yet he's probably still here somewhere
when I need to talk, or need a friend,
or need to be reminded I am loved

As I leave, I look back to see the faeries play
interwoven into my branches that give them a home,
a place to stay, always near me, if you look close
you'll see rainbows in the wings,
the sparkles surrounding the trees,
the glimmers of hope, the letting go
and a new message comes,

It's okay if the branches break, the tree isn't done
there's more life and new direction to go
that wasn't there before, so pause on a limb,
in the in-between 'til a new path opens and
you're brave enough to climb

My path hasn't been tall and straight
yet curvy and broad with complicated bends,
but the tree doesn't see it that way
that's how nature designed him
this is how nature designed me

The forest melodies play
carrying me back to the now
with the rhythm of swaying leaves
and squeaking birds as they converse
the footsteps of squirrels scampering
the gentle drum of acorns dropping

Sprinkled with faeries and
enchanting animals of play,
there's magic in these trees,
a divine connection to land and sky
no matter the shape, no matter the cracks
no matter how I grow—
this way or that

And I carry on
filled with light and love,
my feet grounded again
to God's earth, my connection restored
I smile, in knowingness,
in gratitude, in service
for the light beings in this magical forest.

The Deva of Roses

I'll sit by this wild rose and listen to her stories,
the deva of roses,
she's seen me in all my light
she's seen me in my darkness
she's seen me give myself away time and again

She's seen me receive love with conditions and be okay with that,
she's seen me slip, dropping her leaves to soften my fall,
she's seen me replant and no rose grow—only thorns of the past,
she's seen me lose hope again and again
only to find my way after all the heartache

She's seen me through the eyes of Mother Mary,
Lakshmi, Quan Yin, Aphrodite,
wrapping me in unconditional love,
hoping I realize how different that feels
wondering when I'll turn that love
I so readily give—inward

She's always been there
signs and symbols over the years,
lining my path with her petals, not without thorns,
reminding me in this lifetime
though there's pain and beauty all in one—
there's always unconditional love,
in gratitude, sweet deva.

Deep in the Forest

Where one would expect darkness,
the sun still shines through the pine forest
in glimmers and gleams—
between the boughs of trees,
gloriously pouring through in delight,
reflecting rays falling upon one's face,
creating space to receive in new ways—
a portal of sacred light.

Held by Nature

Here we go again, I show up as I am
feeling unloved, unprotected, undefended

Though you can only love me as deep as I love myself
and for most of the years, that wasn't much

I've found these things deep within myself
I know my worth, my self-love tallies up,
yet I'm still not receiving in the way I deserve

And so,
I go to the ocean and let the sand
hold me in the way I need to be held

I let the sun nurture my body, my soul soaking it all up

I let the water wash away my stream of tears,
so one can't tell where the tears end
and the ocean begins

I let go of my emotions, my brokenness with every shell I toss,
flowing away in the outgoing tide
freeing me up to rise

I whisper my secrets to the moon knowing she'll hold them,
though she already knows them, safe in her crescent

I'll let the dunes show me the cycles of nature
like them, feeling broken and browned—they'll green again,

I'll green again, even if I'm never loved by you

I'm held in nature—
my savior.

The Ancient Forest

This land wasn't meant to be alone,
after the tractor plowed through
after the weeds and vines and trash that accrued,
lit and burnt down to nothing
after the smoke billowed,
this land wasn't meant to stay barren,
it was meant for flowers to grow

Not up the sides of buildings
nor in between sidewalk cracks,
nor where we forgot to trim back
but wild and free amongst
the ferns, the bromeliads, the trees

This land wasn't meant to be alone
it was meant for trees to grow and flourish,
pines and palms, and oaks draped in moss
blanketed together in their own enchanting forest
some even bearing fruit to nourish

The way the trees communicate with each other
their branches reaching toward another
but stopping as they get close and instead
strengthening, creating the most
beautiful, canopied forest

This land wasn't meant to be alone,
it was meant for wild peacocks to roam,
for hawks to perch, for cows to graze,
for coyote packs to move through
the wild jungled maze

Strays finding their way to your wooden porch,
slipping through the lines of bamboo outside your door,
grateful for your presence, though they were here first

This land wasn't meant to be alone,
it was meant to hold your light
to restore your nervous system
until you could reignite

A space for you to feel
safe, nurtured, and held

And just as you can feel your light again
the land glistens and gleams,
the backyard birds return in chorus
for your presence
brought new light
to the ancient forest.

No Worries

The blue jay doesn't spend his lifetime
worrying if the hawk will eat him

He doesn't spend his days worrying
how well his wings work

He flits from branch to branch,
serving his beautiful purpose here on earth

His chirps, trills, whispers
gentle reminders to blissfully be

To come back to oneness
to bask in serenity
to set the worries free.

My Tree

You didn't split into two,
you didn't break,
rather you embraced
the space between to spread and grow,
reaching out for more than you could have
if you grew straight up,
the bends and turns are placed perfectly
the labyrinth of your life,
held in the story of the old oak tree
as your eyes trace the branches,
connecting and grounding what you
are ready to release,
as you repeat
I am not my mistakes
I am not what happened to me
I am worthy of love
I am worthy of blessings
I am complete and whole
in the eyes of my creator,
in the eyes of my own,
in the eyes of the old oak.

From the Leaves

When the leaves drop as they must do,
learning to take the season as it comes to you
instead of resisting the fall, the tumble;
it's a cycle, as natural as the world that surrounds;
you can't hang onto the same tree,
gracefully surrender to the fall, the flow, the circle
knowing it's just a season—
you will regrow.

Healing

Each day filled with sunshine, birds,
connections to the natural world,
connections to God, the palm trees
for which I am surrounded

His love, my love, my worth,
knowing the palms were whispering to me
secrets I never knew sparked by all divinity,
lining my path when I had long been in the dark

Fronds fanned as beams of the Sun
for which they are the same,
fronds fanned for the entry of His Son,
as he went from town-to-town
with a promise of hope and joy

The subtleties of the palms awakening me
as I hold them in my hands,
remembrance of love and adoration,
the *palm* trees, the *palm* of my hand,
a fresh realization

There's healing and magic in
newfound connection,
sourced through divinity—
some discovered, some waiting to be found

The light pours through my palms
a fraction of what could be, just so much
that I can handle at this time

The palms, the sweet, sacred palms
holding loving space for me,

Overjoyed to be in my light
as I am to be in theirs,
we are one—
connected again,
this lifetime sparked.

Feathers of Blue

From window to window
a bluebird fluttered,
as I dusted the lonely rooms
each time I neared the glass
flying around the perimeter of the house,
until he had my attention at last

I stopped to notice, to really notice,
and he stopped too,
sitting in a branch inches away
the other side of the window pane,
his feathers vibrant and bright—
the most beautiful pattern printed across,
showing God really is the most amazing artist

I stood in stillness and gazed
wondering what this busy bird had to say,
a simple, *you are loved*
I heard before he flitted away
a sadness fell over me as he departed,
a sadness I felt before,
as I peered through the window
hoping he was still there

Instead, I saw the most beautiful feather
left under the tree,
the same shade of blue
as the eyes of my brother,
who departed long ago—
a simple reminder
he's still with me.

Flowing with the River

When you feel stuck
think of the waters of the river—
how they flow, naturally
meandering around each curve,
shaping the landscape unknowingly,
sometimes gentle, sometimes strong
yet always flowing, moving, journeying
without so much a sigh

Our bodies made of water,
every bit but the last quarter,
and whenever we feel stagnant—
remember we aren't a puddle on the asphalt,
we aren't the pond where the hawks prey,
we aren't the stream that dribbles and dries,
nor the canals with dams underway
yet we are the powerful river,
with the ability to move naturally

When we flow with what comes,
instead of resisting, combating, analyzing
yet flowing and adapting,
it's much easier to glide

Taking the curves gracefully
letting the current guide the way,
flowing through the seasons,
the melodies each place brings
moving with the rhythm of the water—
an invitation to let go of the outcome
into the flow of creation.

Lowcountry

The universe speaks to me in sunsets, and cats that didn't used to bother with me, now following me,

The universe speaks to me through the cows dipping their heads through the wooden fence

She speaks to me in the space between the clouds,
where the sun drops behind, creating a glow that makes even darkness shine

She speaks to me through the water, as waves gently lap out,
swaying the neon grasses lining the marsh,
the most beautiful dances

She speaks to me in the high-pitched laughter
of my daughter when the barnyard cat rubs against her

She speaks to me through the glow of the moon,
pulling out the emotions that are no longer home

She speaks to me through the cool breeze after a blazing day,
reminding me of the childhood nights when I never felt more alive

She speaks to me with little rainbows through the window panes,
reflecting on the mundane, bringing compassion and love to my gaze

She speaks to me through the tears in my eyes, puddling when divinity comes through, some get a spirit chill, I get eyes that are full

She speaks to me through the songs of my son,
his words, his gifts, connected to God himself

She speaks to me through the sound of locusts
humming in frequency, upgrading mine

She speaks to me through my smile, restoring it to its glory days

She speaks to me through the branches of the trees, waving back and forth as the sun weaves and I catch the twinkling cross,

She speaks to me through all the things that fill my heart,
once I slowed down enough to notice,
to listen to hers, more felt than anything else,
the subtlety, the softness, the love—
of the language she speaks
so gratefully received.

This Rocky Plane

Laying on the beach with arms overhead
ballerina pose across the sand

My heart filled with gratitude for all
the ways nature has held me

The way the mountains held me when I was weak
the way the moon showed me how to rest

The way the leaves showed me how to release
the cycles, the seasons garnering new growth

The way the sun showed me to keep rising even in overcast
the way the rain taught me to stop holding emotion
until it storms

The way the trees whispered to me
secrets of how we are the same

Bridging heaven and earth
on this rocky plane.

The Night Sky

Amidst our adolescence,
we wrapped ourselves in conversation
underneath the golden crescent moon
when my tears streamed,
over what I can't remember
yet as I tried to hide,
you gently advised
to honor all the feelings
not just the *good ones*

Time slowed
as I clung to your words,
even my tears froze mid-flow
yet the stars blinked and blinked
in alignment with this pure consciousness,
so different than what I had been shown
a whole new thought pattern to hold

Ahead of your time
drawn to your angelic wisdom
side-by-side for the summer
starry-eyed, gifts to unwind
the start of my spiritual path
in the form of someone admired

Wishing I took your advice to heart
years of people-pleasing to fit the mold,
carrying more emotion than I ever showed
living inauthentically, unsafe to just be me,
a lifelong pattern tough to unfold

You and I depart yet the messages kept coming
like a warm gentle breeze, up to me to listen

Fast forward
many rides around the sun,
when the grackles came
with their whistles and croaks
the bird of expressed emotion
showing me what I had finally left,
my feelings safe to surface and release,
new patterns form
with so much debris gone

Singing loud and long
stepping into who I'm meant to be,
the memories were breadcrumbs along the way
and guidance moving ahead,
each experience for a reason
the joyful, the uneasy, the sweet ones

The same moon
that shined on me then
shines on me now, the same starry sky,
gleaming and blinking in recognition
seeing me as I am

Just as the stars connect
to make something even greater,
so do we

Connecting the dots of our life,
not society's markers driving success,
but times when we gained wisdom,
turning points that left us broken,
rising up from nothing,
the moments that moved us higher
all connect—
even the seeming outlier

Just like Apus, Orion, and Ursa Major,
we are each a beautiful constellation,
made of stardust, divinely guided by our sacred creator,
showing our journey even greater than we realize,
each time we look up we are no different
than the stars that blink back, patterns and paths
mirrored right back, our steps on earth bringing light
to our journey, this planet, our life,
like stars in the night

When you see them twinkling
as they will do, know they are blinking
in love, in recognition, in joy—
a true reflection of you.

Sacred Shapes

If I could trace the circles, the shapes,
the figure-eights the butterflies
and dragonflies make
as they flutter delightfully—
their patterns and frames
lovingly wrapped around me
I am cloaked in sacred geometry.

Not to Dim

Walking along the one-way road
as the fiery pink hues go for a ride
across the evening skies—
the sun going out with a bang

Always a hidden message
should you open enough to listen,
the sun doesn't try to hide,
she takes up space as she shines
her power felt—a fireball in the sky,
bringing light to dark
making our life possible

And each night as she settles
her orange waves line the skies,
the messages intertwined
reminding us to be in our power,
to take up space, to shine
for the light that we are
not to dim, not to dim for anyone,
not to get caught up in cloudy days,
even in overcast the light is still there

Each morning she rises, as we rise
she ignites something in us
the same power we are both made from—
stardust.

The Only Language I Speak

Tell me the secrets of the stars
the only language I speak
remembrances of before—
dancing in the star's mystique.

Cosmic Dust

Made from the birth of stars
with a past that goes beyond time,
we shine, each at different paths in our soul's growth
the wonders of the sky face us, reflect us, are us
our journeys not so different at all—
nebulas in the sky

Remembering deep within ourselves
every experience, lifetime, season
affects who we are in this moment
learning the lessons we set out,
igniting parts of ourselves we forgot,
greater than we could ever imagine

And just as the nebula in the sky
can be seen in two ways—
as a bright cloud against a dark sky
or, a dark cloud against greater luminosity,
we can either be the light shining in the dark
or we can be the dark with the light behind us.

Sweet Dreams

When the moon is a glowing crescent,
I long to fly up with my softest blanket
nestling inside its cocoon,
falling asleep to the heartbeat of the moon.

Who We Are

When the stars know you by name
and the mountains want to know if you remember
that time you dipped your toes into the river
and knew deep within yourself
there was more to this picture

Honoring your connection to the
water, the dirt, the dust of the stars
knowing there is no separation from
the majestic world that surrounds,
each element holding their stories of us
that go farther back than this
vessel can recall, but the elements
they remember it all

Time and again we show in this place
learning our lessons, going through the motions
we feel broken from, though alive to the natural world
as the elements observe, wondering what it would take
for us to recall—how will it come back? will it at all?

In the moon's glow over the solitude of the trees
in the brisk salty breeze against our cheeks
in the flash of lightning against the shadowed sky
in the palm fronds gently waving as we walk by
in the songbirds flitting through the sunlit branches
in the blushing wildflowers lining the grasses

Their messages echoing through
tuning our frequency to one of love,
remembrance that we've been before and will again
and in those times of discontent

To receive wisdom from the majestic mountains, the warm waters,
the veins of leaves, the fragrance of flowers, the roots of trees,
the sparkle of the sun, the dance of bees,
our oneness radiates so far
that the stars know exactly where we've been,
where we're going, who we are.

My Boy

If you want to feel small and mighty all at the same time
take a step outside to the night sky,
look at the planets you can see with the naked eye—
Jupiter, Venus, the moon, you're looking back in time,
the stars gleaming and blinking,
gas giants and galaxies existing as a tiny speckle
how magical their presence is,
how magical *your* presence is,
all connected in this moment of introspection
your small feet on this planet,
your wide eyes looking up,
how small and mighty you are—
just like the glimmers in the night sky.

My Girl

Ever notice how flowers grow
yet weeds come in faster
to be pulled, to be picked,
yet sometimes they flower
ending up in water cups of my daughter's,
as we wonder why they were ever
labeled weeds when indeed
they were never lesser

Someone somewhere labeled them a weed
and that label stuck,
until a faery goddess came along
and showed them love again—
isn't that how we shift?

Someone somewhere
doesn't believe what came before,
instead, following the beauty that's always been there.

One with Faeries

She runs along the perimeter of the porch
gathering handfuls of wildflowers
the very things others pass up as weeds,
to her, they are the most precious things

In a sea of grass, she finds daisies,
dandelions, and clover, her brother
always amazed asking where her treasure was found
over here, she yells, as she plucks a few more

Sometimes she fills my pockets,
sometimes she throws them to the wind
laughing and spinning joyfully, her chestnut hair
wind-bound as she spins around playful and free

And sometimes she gives them to faeries,
a special spot under the dragon fruit tree
her eyes fill with light, as she gathers
rocks, twigs, adding them to her wild pile
crafting her findings for faery homes and wreaths

My heart is at its fullest as I observe
her immersion in the love that is nature,
her pure heart radiating, her enchanting creations

She brings me back to little me, authentic,
young, free, before the world got the best of me
I'm her mama, but she teaches me more
forever grateful for all the lessons I learn,
she deepens my connection to divinity,
to my inner child who lived so seriously

Mama, come help me make the faery pillows!
I run along, my chestnut hair blowing in my face,
joyful, loved, free, I honor her, she honors me

And beyond the palm trees, under the leaves,
past the pathways well-traveled by our feet
live the faeries, overjoyed to be a part
of this magical retreat.

Rainbow Light

Colors of the rainbow swirl around you
their warmth, their magic, their glow seeping
whichever color you're in need of
comes forth for healing you

Wrapping, filling, igniting
removing lower frequencies,
brightening, strengthening
an infused color wheel unseen

More than just five senses
more than a human body
more than the only place with life,

Where the rainbows render healing
in their sunlit waves

Where the unicorns rest beside,
a journey from the rose-gold skies,

Where the dragons clear the water, the air,
the land with bounteous breaths

Where the gnomes and faeries beneath
the mushroom caps, behind the heart-shaped leaves
carry out their botanical roles
hushed secrets to most

Light-beings, star-crossed skies,
ties to ancient civilizations
twirling around

Interdimensional beings
not limited by physicality
like you and me

Not meant to be seen
their presence felt
giving what's needed

Surrounding you
and if you've forgotten,
surely you'll remember

In the light of the faded rainbow.

Remembering

Spirit child
you were a spirit first
wild and free,
not bound by anything,
at peace in the clouds
blowing with the wind
defying gravity
shape-shifting
sacred-creating
ever-learning
pure energy

Spirit child,
reminders are all around
amongst the soft strength of the trees,
easy flow with the creek,
feathers placed between your steps,
leaves drifting along your path,
sacred geometry that surrounds,
traced by butterflies and bees
all here to remind—
should you look to see.

Inner Child

An old wooden swing,
its ropes tied to the tree,
the swing is moving back and forth
but the seat is empty

The tree calls her back
to what she has forgotten
in the time she took to grow

She took the obligations,
the list of milestones,
her people-pleasing, society-appeasing self
so seriously

The swing still moved without her,
the wind blowing back and forth,
a little sign for her to return

Defying gravity as she once did
in lands far away,
that swing was a reminder—
she forgot to play.

Meeting Again

When we have a lifetime together again,
how will I know it's you?
will our eyes connect
and the stories come forth?
will I remember all that came before—
the joy, the sadness, the hurt,
the move through the karmic lessons,
yearning for when we meet another time,
do we only encounter each other earthside,
or do we meet again in pure love?

Deep-rooted, sweet love,
where we made pacts to repeat
and now I understand how hard it was
to say goodbye, neither feeling and freeing
as we reluctantly let go of the tie
that ran as deep as our souls in that time of need
when the universe obliged,
promises do come true—
the sweetness of love
across lifetimes renewed

Placed together, amidst the chaos
we had moments to treasure
before your silent departure,
when you continued to guide
from the sky instead of earthside,
still traveling together after all this time

Will I remember the separation between land and sky?
that took me decades to realize—
our connection didn't diminish
but rather strengthened,
will I remember how
I waited for your messages to me

savoring every word
wishing they came more naturally?

Will I remember the beautiful gift of knowingness,
how you and I are both serving our divine purpose,
the change-makers in our family line,
the conversations we had all the time,
not realizing how real it became,
not realizing our connection
didn't stop when you left this terrain,
so many years it's been,
when it all washes away again,
how will I know it's you?

When you heard my name
and knew sight unseen
that our names, our bodies,
our souls, would beautifully
intertwine in this lifetime,
the most distinguished high beam,
without so much as seeing,
your eyes have always been your
softest sense, but will you know again
come the next?

At the honey store
when I asked if I had known you before,
and you placed your hands on your heart
the same way mine were held,
and in that moment, it was felt
we had a lifetime or two before,
crossing paths the universe came through
bringing her magic, igniting the light
through us to bring
more alive for all

And as I tell these stories of remembering
I'm clear I'll know it's you,
in the way our eyes meet, in the
words you speak, by the way your
hands move, I'm sure I'll know it's you

Yet, how will I know which story is ours?
how will I know how to untwist the wires?
which page to continue? which chapter to
go back to? how will I know all that came before?
will I even remember there's more?

The book is thousands and thousands of years old,
worn and yellowed pages, but the words are missing,
invisible to our earthly eyes,
only versed through the heart's gaze

Yet the heart doesn't hold the words,
the stories, the places we've been—
only what we felt, blurry remembrances
of what came before don't seem like enough

My deep desire to know
so I can be awed by the magic of the universe,
how when each string untwists,
there's nothing left dangling
all connected in loops and bends
each story magically connected to the next,
each person, each place connected
with purpose

Those that surround
I've danced with before
our stories extend past the edge of time,
some eye-opening, some bitter,
beginnings, endings, sweet, sour,
as they were meant to be

but one thing I'll always look at astoundingly,
how the universe provides magic
for those with believing eyes
and believing hearts
because what fun would life be without
a bit of enchantment inside

When I see you again, as I will,
we'll pick up where we left off,
honoring our hearts, however that looks,
for the true purpose of our soul's growth
in our magical universe,
everything we hold inside of us
sparking something in someone else,
basking in the knowingness
we've danced before and will again—
treading softly, learning our lessons, living in love

And so, I'll trust,
I'll trust the stories to unfold
as they are meant to be,
filled with gratitude that our
paths crossed timelessly,
smiling with the universe
at her beautiful synchronicities.

Who I've Been, Who I Am

Sitting on the park bench on a warm, breezy evening sits a man with a turban wrapped around his head, fastened with jewels from another time, seemingly displaced, he looks up to the magic of the stars, wondering how he can bring that magic in, not realizing the magic is him.

The young bride opening gold-plated chalices squealing in delight, as she enters a seemingly happy life, yet what does a fancy dish have to do with happiness? She already holds the worth she's looking for within herself.

An elephant in the corral, draping her trunk out, thinking she can safely feel the wild from here, but not really because she's in the stall. Scared to swing open the door, but the wild is where she belongs.

The girl with the puffy dress, squeezed into the hourglass shape, as it pinches and pulls, thinking she has to follow the rules, stay in the box, the fancy snow globe, round and round it goes, with a smile on her face as she waves wishing she was any place else.

The artist painting on the streets, splotches of color upon his table, each thing he touches an invigorating mosaic, yet he spent his life feeling he was never enough, stuck in the mind warp of basic.

The turtle poking out his head, unsure of the land, wondering if he should return to the sea, yet there's joy in both places when he sets the fear free.

The retired drill sergeant who once ran a tight ship, the marker of success his hypervigilance, his strictness his asset, now trying to live a life of leisure, but he can't drop the old mindset.

Each of these all the same, not realizing the power within. We are the key we didn't know we held, we are the endless fountain to draw upon, the limits, the cap, the ceiling isn't where we thought.

If we can step out of the known, the logical, the reason, and embrace the messages coming, releasing former versions of ourselves, tending to the inner child healing, remembering our power, our connection, then we can go farther than we ever knew with that one piece of information, long overdue—the magic is you.

Divine Grid

All of these trees are perfectly spaced
as if man planted them on a grid,

but what if I told you that this
was the work of the squirrels, the wind,

the sun, the earth, your footsteps,
for our work and the footprint of the earth

is so perfectly aligned with divinity,

one can't tell where one ends

and the other begins.

Rising Up

While on top of the last hill I climbed,
I saw a perspective so different
than the one from the ground,

I stood and soaked in the ways
of the birds and butterflies,
so I remember when I go back down,
to keep rising up.

The Last to Know

These are the days you dreamt about,
living what you once envisioned
enjoy the magic, sweet child,
and leave behind the stories of yesterday

You are not *who* came before you
You are not *what* you were afraid of becoming
You are pure magic

As you unwind,
the more you step into this life
the more you feel into who you are,

Let it magnify into greater—
the greater that you already are.

Extraordinary Inner Light

The sun rising behind
the light falling around her
forming a halo of sorts
reminiscent of lifetimes past,
memories held
in the light of the rainbow
in the veins of the leaf
in the roots of the tree
gradually seeping through,
moving the forgotten forward
as she steps into all she is meant to be.

Acknowledgments

To my husband—my first audience to all my poems, all my stories, and all the versions of me that came before. You were the first to ever see beauty in my writing, a gentle nudge laying roots for all this to grow, many moons ago. Your unwavering love, kindness, and pure heart provide gentle ground for all of me to land upon. I love you forever.

To my children—the greatest gifts God has ever blessed me with, you have flooded my heart with more love than it has ever known. You inspire me each and every day as you live in your light and authenticity. You bring so much joy to me and those around you just by being you. I could write a thousand books, and none of them would quite encompass the love I hold for you.

To Dennis—my brother, my guiding light. Thank you for the laughter, the love, your long-lost notes, and your presence in my life. I hold you and our memories—before and after—so closely in my heart.

To Shelley—I wouldn't be where I am without you. You've helped me pick up the fragments of myself, my life—and turn them into magic. You have been the bright light shining on my path so I could see the stones placed in front of me. I am eternally grateful to you.

To Megan— the sweetest friend you are, you've been with me through the paths that didn't fit and then the ones that did. You have a heart of the goldest gold there ever was, and your friendship has been one of the most beautiful of my life. You endlessly inspire me.

To Bill and Cynthia—thank you for being so amazing to me, thank you for pouring your love and kindness onto me. Thank you for building me up in my brokenness. Thank you for being exactly what my heart and soul needed exactly when it needed it. Thank you for loving me.

To Akbar and Shirley—thank you for your abundance of love, your ever-present kindness, and your roaring laughter that always makes me laugh even harder. I am grateful to you both for your encouragement and support of my dreams and so much more. I love you forever.

To Shawna—you are always by my side through all the low tides, the high tides, and everything in between. I love that our paths crossed in such a beautiful way this lifetime. You encourage and inspire me every single day. I love you, and I hold our friendship so close to my heart.

To Heidy—thank you for lighting up my life. You are a pillar of love, strength, and compassion, and I am so beyond blessed to know you. You have the kindest heart, share the sweetest words, and encompass the purest love. I love you forever, sweet sister.

To Matt and the Bhakti circle—thank you for the most beautiful platform to have my voice heard. It was your sacred space where I first felt power in my voice and in my words. You saw me when I couldn't yet see myself. You sealed my book-writing dream with *aum,* and it was then I really knew. You have been such a beautiful part of my journey, inspiring me and encouraging me, and I am forever grateful.

To Meadow—you have such a beautiful heart, and I am so honored to know you, let alone call you my dear friend. You were the first one to read my book in its entirety, holding this beautiful space of love and compassion for my entire journey, while weaving in your wisdom. How serendipitous it is that we met! How grateful I am.

To Joe—your light, your frequency magnifies mine with a million reminders of all we are. The space you hold is one of love and remembrance, and for that, I am forever grateful for you. Thank you for reminding me of all that came before when I forget. Thank you for being you, my brother, the magic you are, and the laughter we share.

To Julie—your friendship has been a beautiful, safe space for this healing heart. Thank you for encouraging me, for inspiring me, for loving me, for always being there for me. We shared many sunset yoga practices, where you held space for me to feel safe in this body. Then, our friendship went to the heart and soul. I am so thankful for you.

To my Galway Girls—Fiona, Nicola, Andrea, Clare, Emma, and Trions, your presence in my life was one I will always hold close. You activated a part of my soul that was waiting to come out full force in this lifetime. You showed me love in grief, and you held my heart when it was too heavy for me. I will love you forever and ever.

To Robb—Thank you for your gentle wisdom, thank you for honoring who I am and where I am, thank you for the endless laughs, and thank you for providing so much love and support to me and those I love.

To Amy and Heather—I have enjoyed your beautiful presence in my journey, as you have opened my eyes to more than I could have imagined. I have loved soaking up your magical wisdom.

To Jen, Chris, River, and the Sunflower Club—thank you for the beautiful community to gather and share in. Thank you for holding beautiful space, for heart expansions, and for dreams to evolve. I am so grateful.

To Rebecca Solcer—thank you for your beautiful artwork. You have an incredible gift, and I am honored for your art to connect with my words, my sister from across the seas.

To Chelsie Diane—for sparking in me what was always there. For always being your true, authentic self and helping women all over the world to realign. You are endlessly inspiring.

To Jennifer Sampson—your photography is magical.

And to Mrs. Fattori—the professor who told me I was a writer and plucked me straight out of business school after I had written an essay on how my sunglasses kept me safe and hidden from the world. I hope this book finds you so you can see how far I've come, no longer bound— and it all started... with you.

And, to all the earth angels that have loved and supported me without bounds—I hold your love and kindness so deeply in my heart.

About the Author

Writer, poet, and storyteller, Eileen Anne is the author of *Extraordinary Inner Light,* a book of poetry about healing trauma and realigning with self. With decades of writing experience, Eileen has a unique, heart-centered voice that shines through her poetry.

Eileen has written her way through her trauma, alchemizing her pain while clearing the path for others to follow.

She began writing poetry as a child, typing verses on her grandfather's desktop computer. Her grandmother, her first supporter, framed her award-winning poems and hung them amongst the family photos.

Few know Eileen began in business school. During a required business-writing course, she met a rebel of a professor who went beyond teaching office memos and into the depths of composition.

Feeling a connection with Eileen's words, this professor greatly encouraged her, eventually poaching her from the business school into the arts. That's when Eileen started to realize her gift of writing, but it took her many years and occupations to come full circle.

Eileen was a beloved middle school teacher in the School District of Philadelphia until she became a mother. She then moved into website creation, web-writing, and SEO.

Eileen graduated *cum laude* from Villanova University as an English major with a focus in Writing & Rhetoric. She also attended the University of Galway in Ireland as a *Connelly-Delouvrier Scholar.*

She went on to graduate *summa cum laude* with her master's degree from Holy Family University, along with her masters plus from Pennsylvania State University and Gratz College.

Since college, Eileen received many accolades for her poetry and academic writing including short stories published in anthologies, yet *Extraordinary Inner Light* is her first book.

Eileen now lives in South Florida, where her office is the beach on a Tuesday morning, under any oak tree covered in moss, the waterfront at sunset, or the coffee shop where the peacocks cross.

She also hosts the local Sunflower Club, a monthly gathering where creatives in the community come together to share poetry, music, and stories. Eileen holds the space, shares her poetry, and allows the magic unfold in others as they share their hearts.

Eileen loves nothing more than her children, her husband, nature, and divinity. She loves to bask in the sun, laughter, a great story, and beautiful friendship, as she holds so much space for those she loves. In addition to writing, she adores yoga, traveling, Bhakti circles, reading, and sharing her heart.

She is grateful to all of her teachers, her earth angels, and to the poetry—her creative outlet that has beautifully weaved itself through her life—her lifeline, her voice, the way she makes sense of her place in this world.

Visit her at www.extraordinaryinnerlight.com or on Instagram @extraordinaryinnerlight.

Praise for *Extraordinary Inner Light*

"A poetry book I can REALLY relate to. Powerful, hard-hitting words that land in the softest way. This is exactly what I needed!"
—ASHLEIGH L.

"Heartfelt. Powerful. Raw. True. Eileen, thank you for these amazing words and sharing yourself with us to help us ALL heal. This book is AMAZING!"
—MEGAN TAYLOR, Blogger and World Traveler

"Eileen is a flawless storyteller. By effortlessly weaving magic within the mundane, she paints a beautiful picture with her words."
—EVE SIMONETTI, Yogi, Poet, Artist

"I am so drawn to the authenticity of these poems. This beautiful collection showcases Eileen's remarkable ability to blend personal experiences with universal emotions. Each line is filled with raw honesty, inviting you to share and walk alongside the journey."
—ERIN L.

"Eileen's poetry is resonant—like a well-struck chord, reverberating with depth and authenticity—words that echo the deepest emotions and shared experience of the human soul, words that hold space, words that bridge the gap between the individual and the collective.

To read Eileen's work is to be seen and understood, to be reminded of something beautiful and profound. I'm incredibly proud that I've had the opportunity to watch her evolve as an artist, and I'm grateful to know that her poetry will touch even more lives and inspire hearts across the world."
—MATT SWANNER, Artist, Musician, Yogi

"Eileen's words feel like a cool breeze on a hot summer day. She is pure magic and her LIGHT shines a loving brilliance to behold. I'm grateful for our soul sisterhood in poetry."
—MARIA TERESA PRATICO-SWANSON, Shaman, Poet

"Each poem crackles and sings with Eileen's indomitable human spirit in the face of life's largest obstacles. Her journey through loss, grief, illness, and loneliness to finding unconditional universal love is an inspiring one. Eileen's 'Extraordinary Inner Light' shines through the pages."
—M. ROSE, Poet and Author of "Kerosene Heart"

"Always so inspiring, Eileen speaks bravely from her heart and shares so deeply what we all have in common—this shared human experience and LOVE."
—MICHELLE LEE, Artist

"Eileen is one of those pure writers whose words hit you right in the heart and flow into your soul, like she knows a hidden part about you and just unlocked that in your chest, even when she may not know a thing about you or your past.

An artist who's brilliant at gaining your presence in the present and whose words can help all feel a healing light. I hope one day you too can hear these words in voice form, close your eyes, and see the vision that comes to life from Eileen's art. You will feel connected to everything outside and inside of yourself."
—BOBBY ROW, Singer, Songwriter, and Musician

"Eileen's poetry is a beautiful journey of a woman connecting to herself, coming into her power and sharing her extraordinary inner light and wisdom with the world.

When she speaks her poems, it's like songs that fill your heart. Can't wait for the audio book!"
—VIRIS

"Eileen dives so deeply into her heart, and it's reflected so richly in her words. Thank you for sharing your heart with us."
—COURTNEY, Therapist, Poet

"Such a beautiful, emotional, deep read! This is the poetry book I didn't know I needed! So grateful to read this!"
—ANONYMOUS

"Eileen's voice, both written and spoken, falls to my ears in a beautiful melody and cadence, creating small waves of emotion that ebb and flow along each verse.

Eileen and her poetry have a soft and bright essence, that are both a true joy to get to know! This book is a unique and beautiful expression."
—BEK JOY OLSEN, Holistic Practitioner, Molecular Hydrogen Advisor

"Eileen's poems saturate us as they flow from the pure, formless wellspring of creativity—into the form of words—carried on the vibration of sound as they embrace our ears & reach the formless in us."
—ROBB FERRARO, Kundalini Singing Bowls

"Eileen's work is raw, grounded, and saturated with visuals of nature. She exposes her feelings and allows the reader a front-row seat to her heart.

I couldn't help but feel connected to her words. Thank you, Eileen for sharing this vulnerability with your readers."
—MAUREEN AKE

"Imagine finding your perfect scent, your distinctive spice, and your connection with a calm voice—it is in this poetry book!"
—RABE COGSIL

"Eileen's writing is a glimpse into her world. It flows so poetically from her hands to her sharing with all us. It's beautiful to witness."
—SANDRA KANTER